ROCK

FEVER

A Classic Rock Journey

By

Peter Turvey

All rights reserved

This work is registered with the UK Copyright Service:
Registration No:263410

Copyright for Evening Mail articles from Mirrorpix 2006

Peter Turvey asserts the moral right to be identified as the author of this work.

No part of this publication may be reproduced, stored in a retrieval system, or transmitted, in any form or by any means, electronic, mechanical, photocopying, osmosis, spaceship, little brown paper things, recording or otherwise, without the prior permission of the author.

This book is sold subject to the condition that it shall not, by way of trade or otherwise, be lent, re-sold, used to prop up a table, buried in a time capsule, or otherwise circulated without the author's prior consent.

This book is dedicated to all rockers.

Re-edited October 2023

Prologue

The followers of classic rock are like a brotherhood and sisterhood. When you meet a fellow rocker there is an automatic connection – like you have travelled the same road. This connection, this common path is what this book is all about. It's that moment when you discover rock for the first time, like Obi-Wan "Ben" Kenobi telling you there is a greater purpose in your life. But instead of becoming a Jedi Knight you become a rocker, the air guitar becomes your lightsaber and your first love becomes your Princess Leia...or Prince Leia depending on your preferred modus operandi.

Once on the classic rock journey there is no turning back, no road map and no destination. It's a lifelong commitment and for that reason I know that people who are reading this prologue will already be there – on the journey with me. Because what I have tried to capture in this book is what it was like growing up in such a fertile period of the rock genesis - the mid to late seventies. It's about the hundreds of thousands of classic rock fans that experienced the birth and growth of classic rock and through which the collective memories and heartfelt emotions bind us together.

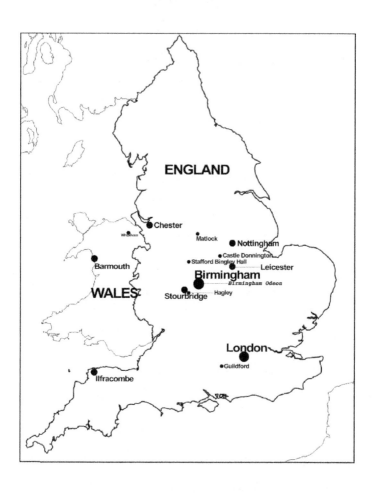

ENGLAND

Chester

Wrexham

Matlock

Nottingham

Castle Donnington

Stafford Bingley Hall

Leicester

Barmouth

Birmingham

Birmingham Odeon

WALES

Stourbridge

Hagley

London

Guildford

Ilfracombe

4

Table of Gigs: 1976 – 1981

(Gigs featured in 'Rock Fever' are in bold)

- 7th Feb 1976 **Be-Bop Deluxe** + Doctors of Madness: Birmingham Town Hall
- 10th April 1976 Camel + Hazzard & Barns: Birmingham Odeon
- 2nd May 1976 **Rick Wakeman**: Birmingham Odeon
- 14th May 1976 **Kiss** + Stray: Birmingham Odeon
- 10th June 1976 Streetwalkers + Dirty Tricks: Birmingham Town Hall
- 5th Aug 1976 **Eric Clapton** + Puppet Show: Birmingham Odeon
- 11th Sept 1976 **Rainbow** + Stretch: Birmingham Odeon
- 16th Sept 1976 **Hawkwind** + Tiger: Birmingham Odeon
- 24th Sept 1976 Budgie + Stray + Strife: Old Bingley Hall
- 8th Oct 1976 BJH + EasyStreet: Birmingham Odeon
- 26th Oct 1976 **Thin Lizzy** + Clover: Birmingham Odeon
- 7th Nov 1976 Wishbone Ash + Supercharge: Birmingham Odeon

- 14th Dec 1976 Steve Hillage + Nova: Birmingham Odeon
- 18th Dec 1976 **Rory Gallagher** + Joe O'donnal Band: Old Bingley Hall
- 2nd Feb 1977 **Lynyrd Skynyrd** + Clover: Birmingham Odeon
- 6th Mar 1977 **Black Sabbath** + Nutz: Stafford Bingley Hall
- 28th Mar 1977 **Pink Floyd**: Stafford Bingley Hall
- 23rd May 1977 **Ian Gillan Band** + Strapps: Birmingham Odeon
- 3rd June 1977 **Rush** + Stray: Birmingham Odeon
- 22nd July 1977 **Moon + Boxer + Crawler**: Birmingham Town Hall
- 18th Aug 1977 **Ted Nugent** + Kingfish: Birmingham Odeon
- 26th Sept 1977 Hawkwind + Bethnal: Birmingham Odeon
- 18th Oct 1977 Bob Seger + Meal Ticket: Birmingham Odeon
- 27th Oct 1977 Steve Hillage + Glen Phillips: Birmingham Odeon
- 14th Nov 1977 Pat Travers + Café Jacques: Birmingham Town Hall

- 18th Nov 1977 Rainbow + Kingfish: New Bingley Hall
- 7th Dec 1977 Mahogany Rush + LoneStar: Birmingham Town Hall
- 11th Feb 1978 **Judas Priest** + English Assin: Birmingham Odeon
- 12th Feb 1978 **Rush** + Tyla Gang: Birmingham Odeon
- 21st April 1978 Rory Gallagher + Joe O'Donnal Band: Birmingham Odeon
- 1st May 1978 **Blue Oyster Cult** + Japan: Birmingham Odeon
- 10th June 1978 UFO + Marseille: Wolv'mpton Civic Hall
- 7th Oct 1978 Wishbone Ash: Birmingham Odeon
- 31st Oct 1978 Budgie + Strife: Birmingham Odeon
- 9th Nov 1978 **AC/DC** + Blazer Lazer: Birmingham Odeon
- 13th Nov 1978 Judas Priest + Lea Hart: Birmingham Odeon
- 9th Dec 1978 Rory Gallagher + Bram Tchaikovsky: NEC
- 23rd Jan 1979 UFO: Birmingham Odeon
- 10th Mar 1979 **George Thorogood** + Ray Campi: Leicester University

- 26th Mar 1979 Bad Company: Birmingham Odeon
- 10th April 1979 **Thin Lizzy** + Vipers: Stafford Bingley Hall
- 10th May 1979 Rush + Max Webster: Birmingham Odeon
- 13th May 1979 Scorpions + Terra Nova: Birmingham Odeon
- 8th Nov 1979 AC/DC + Def Leppard: Stafford Bingley Hall
- 16th Nov 1979 Motorhead + Saxon: Birmingham Odeon
- 26th Nov 1979 **Ten Years After** + Bogey Band: Birmingham Odeon
- 20th Dec 1979 AC/DC + Pirates: Birmingham Odeon
- 7th Mar 1980 April Wine + Angel Witch + Sledgehammer: Birmingham Odeon
- 9th Mar 1980 Gillian + The Broughtons: Birmingham Odeon
- 17th April 1980 Sammy Hagar + Riot: Birmingham Odeon
- 27th April 1980 Saxon + Lautrec: Wolv'mpton Civic Hall
- 31st May 1980 Krokus + Girlschool + Angelwitch: Birmingham Odeon
- 7th June 1980 **Iron Maiden** + Praying Mantis: Birmingham Odeon

- 9th Aug 1980 Ted Nugent + Wild Horses: Birmingham Odeon
- 16th Aug 1980 Rainbow + Judas Priest + Scorpions + April Wine + Riot + Saxon + Touch: **Donnington Rock Festival**
- 23rd Oct 1980 AC/DC + Starfighter: Birmingham Odeon
- 15th Nov 1980 Triumph + Praying Mantis + Dedringer: Hamm'smth Odeon
- 24th June 1981 Diamond head + Silverwing: Stourbridge Town Hall
- 24th May 1981 Girlschool: Torquay Town Hall
- 22nd Aug 1981 AC/DC + Whitesnake + Blue Oyster Cult + Slade + Blackfoot + More: Donnington Rock Festival
- 2nd Sept 1981 Michael Scheckner + Starfighter: Wolv'mpton Civic Hall
- 4th Dec 1981 Rory Gallagher: Birmingham University

PART 1

Chapter 1

Learning to Play the Guitar: Part 1
(1981: Age 19)

I can't remember which night it was, but I do know it was the summer of 1981. I was dreaming.

I was sitting in a dressing room. I'd made it. I was famous. Rich beyond my wildest imagination. I looked at the table...Jack Daniels. I picked it up and drank it neat from the bottle. I felt on fire. I looked around. The room was full of close friends. And women. Lots of women. Ten minutes I heard somebody shout out. I stood up. I was buzzing. I cast my mind back to how it used to be. Before I became famous. I didn't have much and I wanted so much more. I put my hands in the air. I felt so alive. And then, I started to cry. Tears of joy.

That's when I woke up, tears flooding down my face. The dream had seemed so real. It sent a shiver down my spine. And then. The Eureka moment - I finally felt like I had an end product for my passion - I was going to be a rock guitarist with a libido that went up to 11. That was my destiny and now I was going to fulfil it. Tomorrow I would go out and buy my first guitar and unpack my dreams.

The following day I strode purposefully off into the nearby town of Stourbridge (South of Birmingham) to buy the key to my soul.

Bringing your first guitar home is a very nerve-racking experience. First of all you have to introduce it to your parents and hope they like it. Unfortunately their normal reaction is to be shocked and react as if you have brought Beelzebub round for a cup of tea. I remember that *twisted* moment well. "What's that sick, repulsive electric twanger." Dad shouted. "I worked on a lathe in a Birmingham factory for 12 hours a day and you, what kind of a boy are you…you do nothing, you *are* nothing…"

At this point I'd switched off, but I guess he did have a point. But hey I would prove him wrong.

Undeterred I took my guitar up to the sanctuary of my bedroom to comfort it and give it a female name, because that's what BB King did with his guitar, Lucille. I called mine Layla. It had been love at first sight in the guitar shop. It was a pristine black Gibson copy, manufactured by the *world famous* Avon guitars. She was the most gorgeous, most shapely, most perfectly formed guitar I had ever seen. From now on I would eat, breathe and sleep with my Layla and really make something of my life.

Oh yes, I was in deluded ecstasy.

So it was that Layla lay on my bed and purred at me. So I reached out to her and held her close. And that's when it all started to go wrong. Layla was stubborn, Layla was mocking, Layla, to put it bluntly was a right pain in the arse. Arguments would soon ensue and, when Layla flatly refused to reproduce anything resembling a musical tune, that was it. I'd practiced for 5 minutes and I was through with her. So

I ceremoniously carried her to the loft and packed away my dreams for a couple of decades.

For other *guitarists* with more patience than me, their relationship with their first guitar may be a more enduring one. But alas their first love will invariably start to age and look a bit dated and sound a bit droning and inevitably they will be replaced by a fresh and exciting new model with a much better body and tone. Eventually you will see all the old washed up guitars looking for customers at places like Cash Convertor – offering themselves at low prices – desperate to find their Richard Gere and become a Pretty Woman one more time.

****

Summer 1982: One year after the purchase of my first guitar

I was in my bedroom, writing the words for an advert I was going to put in the local paper.

> "For sale, black Gibson copy, great condition, hardly ever used. £50"

I didn't know whether to castigate myself or congratulate myself. Castigate myself for my lack of dedication and application or congratulate myself for my breath-taking level of blind naivety. At no point in my life leading up to the purchase of my first guitar had I ever shown the slightest bit of dedication to anything of a practical nature. Why then had I believed so wholeheartedly that I would become a guitar practising junkie I will never know. I had no musical knowledge whatsoever and any flute playing or triangle hitting I'd done at school had not even registered in my soul.

I was totally clueless. And clueless combined with 'dedication-less' was a formula for certain 'guitar loft-fodder'. For some reason, it never crossed my mind to have a lesson. Oh no, that would have been admitting a lack of innate ability; admitting that perhaps I wasn't born with a silver guitar in my mouth. I'd had Layla for a year and when I'd occasionally taken sympathy on her and retrieved her from the loft I had just used her as a glorified air guitar. I hadn't even learnt a single chord. It was time to send her to a home where she would be more appreciated. The new owner turned out to be some kid from Stoke-on-Trent who wore a top hat. I think his name was Saul Hudson. He told me that one day he would be in the biggest band in the world…poor deluded kid. I wonder what happened to him and my Layla.

Chapter 2

The Gig Scene
(1976 – Age 14)

One of the great things about the gig scene in the mid to late '70s was that there was a good number of superb small venues where the top bands played. There was none of the big venue – how shall I put it - crap, that is so prevalent with today's bands. You can never really get a feel for a band playing live in a big stadium; yes you can experience an atmosphere, but watching a gig from a video screen, because you're so far away from the stage (and pay between £50 and £100 for the privilege) is a different kind of atmosphere from my era. In my day you could be a few feet from the stage and if you were lucky, for example, at a Rainbow gig you would get a sharp piece of Richie Blackmore's guitar shrapnel right in your eye (as he smashed it on stage). Yep, it was about having fun, but an innocent, fresh kind of fun.

Okay, admittedly the rock scene became a victim of its own success and groups were obsessed with who could fill the biggest stadium and who had the most lorries to carry their equipment, but before that there was much more of an affinity between bands and fans. The Birmingham Odeon accounted for a large percentage of the gigs we went to. The original seating capacity was 2,439 with 1,517 in the stalls and 922 in the circle and it had a special kind of atmosphere. The upstairs bar area was carpeted and very 1970s - people would sit on the floor in little groups drinking ale and assessing who had the most concert patches on their jacket.

TOWN HALL, BIRMINGHAM

JOHN SMITH ENTERTAINMENTS presents

BE BOP DELUXE IN CONCERT

plus Guests THE DOCTORS OF MADNESS

SATURDAY, 7th FEBRUARY, 1976,
at 1930 hours

GROUND FLOOR £1.65

PLEASE RETAIN
LATECOMERS will not be admitted until a convenient
break in the programme. Tickets cannot be exchange
money refunded.

Be Bop Deluxe - 7th Feb 1976 *(My First Gig)*

(Birmingham Town Hall, £1.65, Ground Floor, Seat C19)

Exactly 4 months and 1 day before this gig I had been a 13 year-old bedroom headbanger. Now I was ready for the hard stuff. I was already an addict and there was no turning back. But I was only on the soft stuff and I needed a mainline injection - I needed to try an actual gig. I knew where I could get a hit from and the supplier was going to be Be Bop Deluxe. Now you may be desperately leafing through your list of classic rock bands, wondering where Be Bop Deluxe are. Well the truth is, Be Bop seemed to have an identity crisis and in that respect, it was difficult to pin a label on them with any degree of confidence.

However, as a vehicle to achieve my first gig they were perfect. They didn't come with any tales of devil worshipping or drug abuse but instead provided a smokescreen on which a recently turned 14 year old could pitch his request for a night out in Birmingham.

"All right, you can go" my Father acquiesced after I showed him a picture of Be Bop Deluxe in suits and hair that had clearly come into contact with a comb.

From what I had heard (and it wasn't much) they sounded half-decent. A good blues-based guitar sound and somehow I had an attack of scotoma and ignored the fact they looked like a pop band.

I didn't have a clue what to expect. For the younger readers of this book I need to explain what it was like back then. No internet, no rock radio stations, virtually no rock on TV and virtually no rock music in the charts. You went to gigs not knowing what to expect. And in those days when you entered the theatre it was like entering an Aladdin's cave of unknown treasures. Treasures that came in the form of atmosphere, loud guitar, dry-ice, great lighting, loud guitar, thousands of fellow rock heads, loud guitar and of course, rock-chicks! To this day I still have many of those wonderful cerebral treasures.

The Gig

I went to this gig with a mate called Kev. As we stood outside the Town Hall we were aware that apart from the odd kid who was with his parents, we were definitely the youngest there and it just added to the excitement. Just over 2 hours later we were stood outside the Town Hall feeling like two fourteen year olds who had just discovered the meaning of life. The gig was sensational. The guitarist, Bill Nelson, suit or no suit, comb or no comb, was awesome, an absolute wizard on the guitar.

"That was absolutely, absolutely, absolutely mind-blowing; the best ever – nothing will ever top that." I said with my usual level of understatement.

"Holy Shit!" Kev was in shock – joyous shock.

I felt like all my nerve endings were on fire "What a bloody guitarist...I've never seen anything like it...it was absolutely mind blowing." Excitement, like old age, has a knack of making you repeat yourself over and over again.

"Holy shit!" Kev's eyes were alive with the post gig adrenaline

"Mind blowing" I was still repeating myself

"Did you see that at the end?" My voice was racing with excitement, "setting his guitar alight...that was just absolutely mind-blowing. What a gig, nothing will ever top that."

"Holy shit!"

We had both been totally blown away with the sheer energy, excitement and atmosphere of our first live rock concert. The combination of a third row seat and the confines of the Birmingham Town Hall had made it feel like the band, crowd and venue had all merged into one. The whole gig just passed in a whirl of unbridled energy – it had been a truly breath-taking experience. Bill Nelson may not have looked like your typical rock lead guitarist (and singer) but his stage show sure sounded like the real deal. But don't take my word for it, have a listen – start to finish - to 'No Trains to Heaven.'

Evening Mail Reviews

Throughout this book you will be able to read actual reviews from many of the gigs that are featured. The reviews are from the Birmingham Evening Mail. I found them on microfiche at the Birmingham Library. Unfortunately the quality of the photocopies was not brilliant, so I have transcribed them word for word (including grammatical errors). They make interesting reading, not least because quite often the Evening Mail would send reporters to a rock or heavy-metal gig who obviously had very little interest or knowledge of the genre. For example:

- Rainbow: 11th Sept 1976, Birmingham Odeon.

"This was music for a generation happy to flirt with the risk of temporary brain damage."

- Thin Lizzy: 26th Oct 1976, Birmingham Odeon.

"The last British rock band to have such a devastating effect on audiences were Status Quo, who until now have been unrivalled in the field of out-and-out rock."

- Judas Priest: 11th February 1978, Birmingham Odeon.

"About 200 people charged to the front of the stage. I thought the ice-cream lady had arrived. She hadn't. All that happened was that the lights had gone out and Judas Priest had come on."

- Blue Oyster Cult: 1st May 1978, Birmingham Odeon.

"Blue Oyster Cult are like a grittier yet more sophisticated version of Status Quo."

- AC/DC: 9th November 1978, Birmingham Odeon. "Their style is way out of date, Zeppelin were doing this years ago."

Review from the Birmingham Evening Mail

Be-Bop on the right road

Be-Bop Deluxe, Birmingham Town Hall

The flaming guitar, held triumphantly aloft by Bill Nelson like some kind of sacrifice to the audience was really unnecessary.

Be-Bop Deluxe had already proved themselves.

Be-Bop have been heralded as one of the bands most likely to succeed this year. After watching them on Saturday night I'm convinced they will be.

The flashy guitar stunt slightly dimmed what had been an evening of enlightenment.

The band's new album, "Sunburst Finish", contains some fine material, but it is a rather cold piece of work. Be-Bop Deluxe live though, are totally different. On stage they are vibrant, especially lead guitarist Bill Nelson, the band's songwriter.

The precision and excellence of Nelson is matched by the other members – Simon Fox on drums, bass players Charlie Tumahai, and keys man Andy Clarke. They work as a very solid tight unit, though the star of the band is undoubtedly Nelson, and he obviously enjoyed the spotlight's glare.

His songs smack a little of Roxy Music at times, but the group's talent is there to see.

Doctors of Madness, support band, are rather strange. Their music is very aggressive and occasionally frightening.

But they also possess a high degree of musicianship which allied the theatrics of their act, could put them on the same road to success as Be-Bop Deluxe.

KEN LAWRENCE

Tribute to Kev

Kev and I would eventually drift apart when we left school. It's strange how really strong friendships can sometimes fade away. It's like you have an unscripted, valedictory moment; no ceremony, no farewell speech, just a point in your friendship when your road forks and without a word you go your separate ways. That's how it was with Kev and (when I left school in 1978) it would be over 30 years before I would hear his name again.

I'm sure I bought a single by Witchfinder General in the 1980s. They were part of the New Wave Of British Heavy Metal that you will read about later and the single was released on the independent label Heavy Metal Records. If I did buy it, I don't have it now. How strange to think that 30 years later I would find out that my old mate Kev was a bassist in that band (I didn't even know he played the bass!). And an influential band as well as they have been cited as a major influence on the doom metal genre. Kev went by the interesting nickname of "Toss." Not a clue where he got that from. Apparently he was in the group from 1981 to 1982. I'm receiving all this information second hand because very sadly Kev died on 20th Dec 2008. I was numb.

My memory of Kev is preserved in time and the fossilisation of that memory is the joy we shared as we exited the Birmingham Town Hall on 7th Feb 1976. Rest in Peace Kev.

So that was my first gig. The next day I eagerly reported my experience to my mates Huw, Steve and Paul. I was hooked and I wanted more and my increasingly animated and exaggerated review of the gig: *"....the encore was a 20 minute guitar solo and then he set his guitar alight and then he sacrificed a virgin"* meant Huw, Steve and Paul wanted it as well. I looked for the next hit. I was up for going to every rock gig that came around, but with a broad range of rock tastes amongst the lads, each gig had to be sold on its individual rock merits. For example, take progressive rock. Steve wasn't a big prog rock fan. But because this style of rock was considered the more technical and intellectual brand of the genre, if there was any negativity to a proposed gig, all I had to do was utter the put-down 'you rock-dummy' and that normally sold it. But as I say, each gig needed a slightly different pitch.

After school in Stourbridge – mid April 1976

Huw, Steve and I had met to wander the streets.

"Huw, Steve, how do you fancy going to see a rock legend the first Sunday next month?" I had started my sales pitch.

"Who is it?" they said in perfect synchronisation.

I needed to build this one up. I knew Huw would be relatively easy to convince as the artist was part of the prog-rock congregation, but his recent outings to fantasy land meant it was going to be harder to convince the blues-rock influenced Steve.

"He's regarded as one of the most talented musicians in rock and he's now on tour with a massive great ROCK ensemble." I really shouted out the word rock.

"Who is he?" Huw said in a persistent manner.

"What the bloody hell is a rock ensemble?" Steve added.

"Rick Wakeman," I said, as if those two words should be enough to conclude my case for going. I had loved the escapism of Rick Wakeman's solo stuff.

"Rick Wakeman out of Yes?" cried Steve.

"Yes, Rick Wakeman out of Yes," I said in a tone that emanated annoyance for asking such an obvious question.

"Rick Wakeman of the long flowing gowns and strange medieval lyrics?" Steve was obviously making a point that his previous question had not been a question, more a rhetorical cry of exacerbation.

"Yes you rock dummy, Rick Wakeman, one of the exponents of the technical and intelligent side of rock."

I was already reverting to humiliation to try and secure Steve's support.

"Bollocks he is." It clearly hadn't worked.

There was silence.

"How much?" said Huw.

"Quid fifty for a seat at the back," I replied.

"Okay, I'm in." Huw was in.

"Go on then." Steve was also in!

Rick Wakeman - 2nd May 1976
(Birmingham Odeon, £1.50, Rear Stalls, KK39).

Exiting the Birmingham Odeon at 10.30pm we were all smiling.

"Now that was an experience wasn't it" I was really making a statement rather than asking a question.

"Really enjoyed it," replied Steve "Great to see the entire band having a laugh on stage."

"Yeah, but when you're writing whole albums about Henry VIII and King Arthur you're going to need a sense of humour, otherwise you might get accused of being pompous and self-indulgent," said Huw with a wry smile.

"Or just a plain tosser," said Steve with a touching veracity that caused us all to laugh.

"I have to say it was much better than I thought it was gonna be – the time just flew by." I was almost being enthusiastic about a keyboard player!

"Yeah, we'll give you that one Pete." I guess that was a sort of affirmation from Steve.

We made our way to the station in good spirits and boarded our train home. We'd had a good night. We all felt it and we all knew that as Rick and his group weren't the archetypal rock band and because the band didn't take things too seriously, then a degree of dilettantism was necessary. It allowed us to convey clearly that we also had not taken the evening too seriously and missed the point. None of us knew what the point was, but it was important that we hadn't missed it.

As our chatter died down I thought it was a good opportunity to mention an American band I'd heard about, that were playing at the Odeon in 12 days time. I was just about to bring the subject up when Huw piped up:

"So you've seen a suit wearing guitarist and now a keyboard player wearing a cape. What next, a bunch of transvestites?"

"Lads, are you up for going to see Kiss?"

Review from the Birmingham Evening Mail

Rick earns the raptures

Rick Wakeman, Odeon New Street, Birmingham
Nearly 5000 fans can't be wrong – and that's how many saw Rick and the English Rock Ensemble last night.

Rick dominated the centre stage, his long blond hair flowing over a floor length cape, and whirling like a Dervish between innumerable keyboards.

The ensemble helped him do justice to his grandiose, finely-crafted musical pieces, whether about Kings Arthur's court, the wives of Henry VIII or journeys to the centre of the earth.

Musically, there was a fascinating array of textures from keyboards, even though they seemed a little loud.

Ashley Holt's vocals were strong and forceful, John Dunsterville played intelligent guitar and there were soaring, joyous brass section and a lot of varied percussion.

It could have been rather pompous and over-serious, but the band clowned around a lot, and good humour was the order of the night.

DAVID GRITTEN

The Following Night – Huw's House

"Who the hell are Kiss?" said Huw.

"Kiss, they're American, they're coming over here on their first ever tour. We could get some cheap seats at the back for £1.50."

"Are they any good?"

"They have quite a reputation." I was trying to find the right time to mention their 'unique' stage act.

"So have you heard any of their stuff?" Paul enquired.

"Nope, I've heard nothing, but I've read in Sounds (Sounds was a UK rock music newspaper, published from 1970 to 1991) that they have lasers and amazing pyrotechnics and Local Councils are concerned for the safety of the crowd."

"And what did it say about their music?" Steve joined the conversation.

"That they have lasers and amazing pyrotechnics and…" this was the bit that I thought might cause a problem "…no one's ever seen what they look like."

I was hoping that would be enough information, but instead I had just opened up a can of worms.

"What do you mean, no one's ever seen what they look like?" Huw said incredulously.

"Because they wear more make-up and higher heels than your momma does."

"What!" the lads retorted collectively. The phrase was 30 years ahead of its time so I didn't expect them to get it.

"You mean they're glam rock?" I couldn't quite detect whether Paul said this with a degree of excitement or distain.

It was 1976 and the so-called glam image was firmly entrenched in pop music. It had also infiltrated what some would call rock, like the music of David Bowie, T-Rex and Slade, but for it to infiltrate 'proper' rock music or heavy rock was surely an oxymoron...glam and rock in my narrow opinion at that time should never be allowed to cross-pollinate.

One of the things I liked about rock music was the 'dress-code'. I had no sense of fashion, so the challenge of matching a t-shirt with a pair jeans just about fell within my mental capacity. It was simple, I got up in the morning, put on the said jeans and t-shirt and there they would stay for an undisclosed number of days – accessories like soap or a comb never entered the equation. But it became much more than just a fashion statement, it became more of a social comment - that we weren't going to be influenced by social trends and record company-led image fads. We were collectively all individuals and we would never, ever sell our sacred music brand to some flamboyant fashion fad. I hated any brand of music that had 'glam' before its name and so when I heard about Kiss I was in two minds. I was really curious to see Kiss playing live because of all the hype I'd read about their concerts, but I was loath to defend the glamorisation of rock. The only way I could rationalise this conflict in my own mind was to convince myself that Kiss were engaging in something far more subtle – I had no idea what, but leaving a philosophical question mark in the air seemed to do the trick.

"No, not glam rock…more…more…experimental metal," I said wondering where the hell I'd plucked that one from. "Look, forget the costumes and make up, they're a kick ass rock band," that really left a knot in my stomach.

"How do you know, if you've never heard a single track of theirs?" Paul was very sharp.

"Look, how would you feel if you missed the gig in which the Birmingham Odeon burnt down and hundreds of people were burnt alive or 'lasered' to death? If nothing else, we can get the cheapest tickets available and have a laugh and I bet the atmosphere will be great."

Kiss - 14th May 1976
(Birmingham Odeon, Rear Stalls, FF33, £1.50)

This tour was to promote their 1975 album 'Alive!' The tour saw Kiss visit the UK for the first time, taking in three dates: Manchester's Free Trade Hall, Birmingham Odeon and London's Hammersmith Odeon.

Outside the Birmingham Odeon - 10.30pm (Post-gig)

"Interesting," said Huw in a way that conveyed much more meaning to the word.

"Very interesting," agreed Steve.

"Did the bass player have a nose-bleed?" asked Paul.

"Whose idea was that?" they all said together staring accusingly at me.

I thought Kiss were a good stage act...plenty of energy and you could tell that they were giving it their all, but to me their songs weren't that memorable and sadly

36

none of the band were stupid with the flare gun and the place didn't burn to the ground and the Birmingham Odeon had no smoke let alone water.

I read many years later that Kiss got disillusioned after this, their first tour of Britain and vowed never to return. Don't you just hate it when people don't stick to their word? Sorry Kiss fans...only joking...ish.

On the train journey home we went through the post gig autopsy. We were united in our belief that we would never disown our jeans and t-shirt heritage. "This is me," I said with 100% commitment, "I will never, no never, wear anything other than jeans and a t-shirt." Oh, the naivety of being 14...

Seven months later I was waiting at Hagley train station (Near Stourbridge, West Midlands) to meet the lads. We were off to see Steve Hillage.

"What the hell is that?" Huw said, leaving his mouth open to subconsciously emphasise his amazement.

"It's an Afghan." I said with the utmost seriousness. Synchronised laughter ensued.

A few months earlier I had seen footage of Woodstock, with Hendrix and Ten-Years After. The whole atmosphere had looked brilliant and in my impressionable eyes the Afghan wearing hippies looked...well, hip. I was still wearing my jeans and t-shirt and I had simply added to the look.

This was the natural evolution of the dedicated follower of rock fashion: You went from being a jeans and t-shirt wearer – a 'teenager with angst, but no idea why' stereotype; to a 'Neil' (Young Ones) hippie type image, with Afghan and an almost *fanatical devotion* to lentils; then on to the Biker type persona, including leather jacket, no motorbike and an attitude that was angry, but you'd forgotten why.

"Have you taken it for a walk today?" Paul said with his usual impeccable comedy timing. More collective laughter ensued.

Taking oneself seriously, but not that seriously, is an essential part of a rocker's make-up and I joined in their laughter, although it was more feigned than heartfelt. It would be weeks before the beloved Afghan made another appearance.

Rock Music And The Image – Part 1

The image and mythology of rock is part of the (counter) culture of the music. To the followers of rock the connection to the music is absolute; it is intense, heartfelt and emotionally rewarding. The connection to the image is far more metaphysical and bawdy. The stories of bands on the road are legendary. As young fans we loved to lap up the image, because the perception was that it put the rock genre way above any other musical genres in terms of the 'coolometer'. What could be cooler than a life of gigs, beer, women and hotel room smashing? It was rebellious, but it seemed acceptable and fun and it seemed you belonged, even if you weren't there. We saluted the rock gods, just as much for their contribution to the anti-establishment, as their contribution to rock music. They were the custodians of the myth and we entrusted in them to uphold the holy faith and bed a groupie every night, drink Jack Daniels and dispose of perfectly good TVs. But rock fans knew instinctively where the line was drawn in terms of the seriousness of the music against the seriousness of the image. Those that took the image or the lyrics too seriously, fans or non-fans, completely missed the point. Rock filled the gap between the protest lyrics of the hippie generation and the politicised lyrics of the punk generation. The rock generation sung about cars, women, drink, and wizards – it was pure escapism. And, as I had no desires, motivations or ambitions –

other than to become a whisky drinking, womanising, racing driver nicknamed Merlin – it was perfect.

Following the Kiss gig we went to see the Streetwalkers at the Birmingham Town Hall (10th June 1976). They were fronted by the *ex*-Family vocalist Roger Chapman. Great gig, but none of us really knew their music.

I was desperate for someone famous to tour. Eric Clapton couldn't have chosen a better time to go on the road.

Eric Clapton - 5th August 1976
(Birmingham Odeon, £2.80, Centre Stalls, R8)

The lights had just gone down and a big cheer went up. Paul, Huw, myself and Steve were present to see the mighty Eric Clapton. The band began the first song and Eric walked on stage, and I tried to make out what he was wearing.

"What's that on Eric's head?" I shouted to Steve.

"Looks like a potty."

"A potty?" From the centre stalls I could make out that EC had something on his head but I wasn't too convinced about the potty observation.

"Is that a potty on Eric's head?" I asked Huw.

"No, it's a pig's mask."

"A pig's mask?" I was equally incredulous.

My eyes were starting to adjust to the light and sure enough Clapton had walked on stage with what looked like a pig's mask on. To this day I still have no idea why. Perhaps it seemed like a good idea at the time? Perhaps the idea was influenced, ever so slightly, by large quantities of drugs and alcohol? It didn't matter, he could have walked on dressed as Babar the Elephant and we would have still applauded. A couple

41

of slow numbers passed and Eric was noticeably leaving most of the solos to the other guitarist (George Terry).

"Do you think he's alright? He looks a bit spaced out to me," I said to Huw

"Naagghh, he's just enjoying himself," replied Huw. That was good enough for me.

The four of us were sitting in a relatively restrained line as most of the stuff had been bluesy and whilst it was good guitar it wasn't headbanging material. Then, five numbers in, Eric surprised us all by playing *Layla*. We had unanimously agreed that this would be kept back until the encore, so when he started to improvise on the guitar we thought it was the introduction to another blues song – but he was teasing us and soon the notes led into the classic opening riff. *Layla* was one of the main reasons we were there, so on hearing the familiar musical stimuli, the four of us dive-bombed into our headbanging routines. We were well back in the centre stalls and when I looked up to see what was going on I noticed that we were the only ones headbanging. Indeed the older guy next to Steve seemed most displeased with our display. Undeterred I reunited my hair with my thighs and carried on.

When it came to the end of *Layla* Eric started talking to us – the crowd that is – not just us four lads. He seemed to be rambling on about Birmingham.

"What's he saying?" I asked Steve.

"Something about England becoming shrouded in something and I think he's having a go at sodomy – oh, and Enoch Powell is a goat."

Must be spaced out I thought to myself. Eventually Eric blasted out the next song and we thought nothing of his verbal interlude until some years later when we read the following:

'In 1976, Clapton was the centre of controversy, and accusations of racism, when he spoke out against increasing immigration, during a concert in Birmingham. Clapton said that England had "become overcrowded", and implored the crowd to vote for Enoch Powell to stop Britain becoming "a black colony". The photographer Red Saunders wrote a reply, which was subsequently published in a number of papers including the NME and Melody Maker. The letter led directly to the formation of Rock Against Racism.'

Halfway through the gig, Eric told us he had a special guest joining him on stage but he didn't introduce him by name. The crowd erupted when the mystery star walked on.

"Who's that?" I whispered loudly to Huw who was sat on my left.

"No idea, I'll ask Paul."

"He doesn't know either, ask Steve."

"Who's that?" I asked Steve who was sat on my right.

"Not a clue."

"He doesn't know either." I relayed Steve's reply to Huw, who in turn, looked back at the stage, then leant forward and looked down the row to his left and then to his right.

"Ask Steve to ask the guy next to him who the guest star is; he looks like a hardened rocker."

"Ask the guy sitting next to you if he knows who he is." I directed the request to Steve as instructed.

Steve duly obliged.

"What did he say?" I was eager to have this gap in my rock knowledge filled.

"He said yes, of course I fuckin' do." I guess he hadn't forgiven us for our headbanging antics. Undeterred I took in this information without altering my expression.

Huw asked me what the rocker next to Steve had said.

"He said yes, of course he fuckin does," I replied with the level of seriousness to which I had received the information.

Huw duly passed this information on to Paul and we sat there none the wiser as to who the mega star guest singer was.

It was only after reading the gig review in the Birmingham Evening Mail the following day that we found out who he was (see below).

Shortly after the mystery rocker's slot, Eric gave the mike to one of his backing singers in which he told us that he was sure we would all recognise her great voice.

"Huw, who's she?"

"No idea, I'll ask Paul."

"He doesn't know either, ask Steve."

"Steve, who's she?"

"Not a clue."

Steve's 'rocker-mate' was leaning forward and looking menacingly at us all. We silently and unanimously decided to leave the enquiry there.

Review from the Birmingham Evening Mail

Clapton sets great pace

MIDLAND fans of Eric Clapton really got value for their money last night.

In addition to all their dreams coming true by seeing the guitar hero on stage, there was the added bonus of a brief appearance by Van Morrison.

The first number, a track from Clapton's new album, "No Reason To Cry," set the scene for a stunning set by an amazingly together band.

Sergio Rodriguez on percussion and Yvonne Elliman and Marcy Levy providing back-up vocals give Clapton's latest band a really punchy sound, and guitarist George Terry is outstanding.

After a second slower number from the new record, Clapton gave the fans what they really wanted – one of his classics. This was "Layla," the first few notes from Clapton building up the expectation.

The band didn't let anyone down, although it was interesting to see that George Terry was the man behind the best guitar sounds on stage.

Then surprise, surprise, on came Van Morrison to rapturous applause. A slow blues, a rocking version of "Rock Me, Baby" and he left. We could have listened to him all night.

But the band didn't allow pace to slow down. "Tell The Truth" followed with Clapton and Terry battling it out for the title of the best axe man on stage.

After a fine version of the Blind Faith number "Can't Find My Way," by Yvonne Elliman there was, I felt, rather a poor version of "Knocking on Heaven's Door."

The set ended with a slow blues, really the only number in which Clapton did his guitar thing.

Perhaps it's because we have heard so many people play his solos before, but I felt they lacked punch and again I have to say that Terry's guitar playing sounded fresher and more electrifying.

But Clapton can still exchange riffs with anyone, and he has one of the best bands in the land at present.

SANDY COUTTS

Rainbow - 11th Sept 1976

(Birmingham Odeon, £2.00, Rear Stalls, AA9)

It had been a week since the Clapton gig. It was a Saturday morning and the lads were round my (parents) house.

"Lads, I've been thinking..."

"Steady," said Paul as if that quick repost was compulsory.

"I've been thinking...my favourite music is heavy rock and so far I've seen a suit-wearing guitarist, a cape-wearing keyboard player, a make-up-wearing glam rock act, a group nobody's heard of and a blues legend who walked onto the stage wearing a pig's mask. It's about time I saw a proper heavy rock band."

"Go on," said Huw.

"11th Sept, Birmingham Odeon...Rainbow. The box office is open today."

There was a group silence and then, without a word being said, we stood up in perfect synchronisation and headed for the door. We were on our way to buy tickets for our first 'proper' heavy rock concert.

The Gig

For this gig it was the most memorable line up for Rainbow:

- Ritchie Blackmore: Guitar
- Ronnie James Dio: Vocals
- Jimmy Bain: Bass
- Tony Carey: Keyboards
- Cozy Powell: Drums

There was a real buzz of anticipation in the air.

"Are we going for it?" I said. We were still young but we didn't feel like rock concert virgins anymore.

"Absolut…," I didn't hear Huw finish his reply, as just at that moment the lights started to fade and the crowd surged forward like they'd been hypnotically programmed to follow this behavioural pattern whenever the lights went down. I followed suit and Huw and Steve followed close behind me. Those in the expensive seats didn't stand a chance as we poured *en masse* to occupy the open ground between the front row and the stage. We were young, male and we were really up for this gig. It was total darkness and then the sound of Judy Garland's voice told us that she and her friends '*must be over the rainbow, rainbow, rainbow.*' My God, we were so primed - then Cozy hit the drums, Ritchie blasted his guitar, a massive rainbow came alight and then the whole band were lit up on stage.

Outside this environment and away from the comfort zone of the lads, I would be very self-conscious, but at that moment in time if there had been 20 TV cameras pointing at me I wouldn't have cared; I was in a different world.

Cozy brought the opening bars to an abrupt end and the silence on stage was broken by all of us giving a massive cheer and then bang! The spotlight hit Ritchie, then Tony, then Cozy, and then Jimmy. Simultaneously a wall of noise hit us. And then Ronnie screamed the opening words to *Kill the King*. The front of stage mass of testosterone exploded - what a buzz, I just couldn't hold back my emotions, every sinew felt like it was going to explode, I just had to go mental, but the beat was so fast that very soon the crowd were all over the place: people headbanging, people with their hands in the air, people jumping on one another, it was total chaos - sensory overload but boy what a feeling, what an outpouring of connective energy it created. I hadn't had sex yet, but I remember thinking it couldn't possibly be as good as this – clearly the early signs of a worrying devotion to rock!

Huw and I united arms in a show of rock camaraderie that we would never have displayed outside this setting and then Paul jumped up and down behind us using my shoulders for leverage. We hadn't the time or the energy to talk and even if we had it wouldn't have mattered, because the music was so wonderfully loud. Standing by the bass bins we got the full force of the volume and we loved it. How as a species we can feel such incredible intensity of emotions when once upon a time we were just random molecules floating in space I will never understand. Maybe I'll ask Brian May.

Everything about the gig was just magical. We all knew this was our coming of age in terms of rock concerts.

On the train back home we so hyped - all talking at the same time.

"Look…" I pulled an imaginary piece of wood from my hair "it's a bloody splinter from Ritchie's guitar."

We all laughed. The gig had been our first 'guitar smashing concert' and we knew that Ritchie had honoured us that night with a full on performance. On the way to the gig, I had told the lads that Ritchie had a reputation for being a tad temperamental, and that he could well bugger off stage without bothering to play an encore. It had been documented that one night he could play two or three encores, then the next night zippo and I had heard through the grapevine that four days earlier (on the 7th Sept 1976) he had deemed the Cockneys not worthy of an encore and the Hammersmith Odeon crowd went home mentally scarred, wondering why he hadn't smashed up a perfectly good guitar. Apparently no one was ever quite sure what his criteria was in making those decisions. But as I said, that night Ritchie had honoured us with his full repertoire and he left us feeling that life was a magical thing. It had been a raw performance, full of passion and musically we thought they were on another planet. This had been the best yet and now we were helpless rock-concert addicts.

Review from the Birmingham Evening Mail

C'mon feel the noise!

Rainbow, Birmingham Odeon

This was music for a generation happy to flirt with the risk of temporary brain damage.

Rainbow play heavy, thumping monotonous music excruciatingly loud. Perforated eardrums were always a looming danger.

Overall, they are musically limited, though Richie Blackmore is a fast, dexterous guitarist.

The presentation was spectacular, with the back drop depicting a Gothic castle, and a huge arch electronically lit in the colours of the rainbow (in the wrong order).

Cozy Powell's drum solo, accompanying a recording of the 1812 Overture, injected wit and a blinding explosion into proceedings.

But it wasn't really my cup of decibels, and I got bored. But Rainbow got a rapturous reception from a young, mostly male, packed house and you can't argue with that.

DAVID GRITTEN

Chapter 3

Growing Up

I was born at home in 1961. Home was Quinton. Quinton is a ward of Birmingham, 5 miles west of the city centre. When I was three my parents moved to Hagley. Hagley is a large village in Worcestershire. It is 12 miles south west of Birmingham.

(1967: Age 5)

Why do some of us connect with rock, while others are inspired by soul, or reggae or pop music? I believe it's due in a large part to what the music says to you when you're listening to it. Not necessarily from a lyrical point of view, but from something far more transcendental. When I connected with rock in the mid-1970s there was a commonality of disillusionment amongst young people, but the way kids sought their musical outlet for these frustrations manifested itself in a wide variety of genres from northern soul to rock'n'roll. So the connection had to be something far more personal.

Typically (but not exclusively) the psycho-social make-up of a young rocker is someone who can't find a place to fit in life and struggles to interact outside his own comfort zone – there is a sense of direction without direction and purpose without purpose. Ultimately there is an intense desire to be free from the things that we believe prevent us from being who we want to be … an individual. To quote Brian…(talking to the masses).

Brian: "You've got to think for yourselves! You're all individuals!"
Crowd: [in unison] "Yes! We're all individuals!"
Brian: "You're all different!"
Crowd: [in unison] "Yes, we are all different!"
Man in crowd: "I'm not..."

© *Monty Python's Life of Brian*

For me, my psycho-social seeds were sown as young as aged five, when on my first day of Infant School (September 1967) my lack of confidence was severely exposed. I felt like I'd been thrown into a completely unknown territory, with no map or words of advice to get me through it. I just put my head down and survived in my own silent little zone (waiting for rock music to bring me to life). I didn't say a word and such was the intensity of my reaction that the teacher had to call my mother to enquire as to whether I had actually learnt to speak.

Infant School, Playtime

I noticed a familiar face in the playground.

"Hello Huw, what you doing?"

"Just standing. What you doing Paul?"

"Pete."

"Yes, I meant Pete. What you doing Pete?" In synchronisation with his reply Huw scratched his bottom as if to divert my attention from his error.

"I'm just standing."

Yes the conversation flowed just like the old times and we were soon recounting tales of excess and decadence from our days in nursery school. It was really comforting to see an old school friend, even if I was only five. When the bell went for the end of playtime we were already inseparable and it was really comforting when Huw asked me, as we made our way back to classroom, "What was your name again?"

Chapter 4

Growing Up
(Sunday 12ᵗʰ January, 1969)

I was 7, largely unaware of the big wide world. Largely unaware that The Scaffold were number 1 in the UK singles charts with *Lily the Pink.* Largely unaware that this day would later on in my life play a huge part in who I became. Four lads - one from the Black County, one from Redditch in Worcestershire, one from West London and the other from Sidcup in Kent – released their debut album. It was to change the face of rock music forever and ultimately put the 'classic' into rock. The album was the eponymously named debut from Led Zeppelin. Oh yes…what a moment in time.

Chapter 5

Learning to Play the Guitar: Part 2
(The Beginning – Age 37)

6th January 1999 – Back Alley Music, Chester

For a total outlay of £194.99 I got a Fender Squire Strat, a Watson mini amp, a tuner and an easy guide to learning to play the guitar. As far as I was concerned, I was sorted. This time, rock guitar greatness would be mine.

Now I don't mean to be disrespectful to guitar players, but I figured it can't be that hard to play the bloody thing…after all, they make it look so easy. A big mistake, a big, big mistake. Firstly, I had completely blanked out my first attempt to play the guitar in 1981, as if it was too traumatic for me to even think about. And secondly I hadn't entered into my reasoning the 'natural ability' factor or, to be precise, my lack of it; and the age factor or, to be precise, my ever increasing abundance of it. Delusion – a rockers best friend!

When I got back home I excitedly plugged my new guitar into the amp and opened up the 'Easy Steps to Learning to Play the Guitar' book. The first thing the book told me was: *'Within days you will be playing along to a whole host of well-known songs.'*

Brilliant I thought, as *Stairway to Heaven* and *Freebird* came into view of my over-excited imagination. I couldn't wait to get started.

Lesson One: Choosing Your Guitar – Electric or Acoustic? Deeerrrr, that was a difficult one! I wanted to attract a non-stop stream of groupies: what 'effin' use was an acoustic?

Lesson Two: Know Your Guitar. What was I meant to do, say hello to the bugger or give it a kiss? All I needed to know was did it look good? Yes, I'd just bought it. Did it have a ball-breaking sound to it? I wouldn't know till I played it. Lesson two sorted.

Lesson Three: Tuning your Guitar by Ear. I was a beginner, what was the point in talking about tuning my guitar by ear when I had no idea what the notes were meant to sound like in the first place?

Lesson Four: Taking Care of Your Strings. They really were having a laugh.

Lesson Five: Adopting the Correct Posture. I already knew the frigging correct posture: feet about six feet apart, back arched and head tilted backwards – posture sorted.

Lesson Six: Strumming. Strumming was for limp-wristed jessies, not for lead guitarists. Another lesson accomplished.

Lesson Seven: Your First Chord. Chords...now wasn't that something to do with strumming? It didn't sound like it would teach me how to become a guitar neck gymnast, but I thought it was best to give this lesson some attention. After all, I was half-way through the book and I'd only been going ten minutes.

D Major was my first challenge. There was a little information box that informed me that D Major was a happy and bright chord. I guessed that was one the Death Metal boys avoided like the plague. It didn't sound like the sort of chord my heavy metal heroes would go for either, but I persevered. By carefully placing one finger at a time on the fret board (a.k.a., the neck of the guitar), I eventually managed to form the chord shape and then my strumming arm started moving like Pete Townsend: big whirling wheels! It looked good, but what a bloody racket; I turned the pages back to the strumming lesson. I was told to do some simple downstrokes over all 6 strings. The downstroke was represented by the following symbol:

This seemed a bit strange, surely an arrow or a shape like a '**V**' would have been better; in other words, something that pointed downwards; but what was this next to it? It was the **'V'** symbol; now what was it saying? That this symbol represented the upstroke, but the bloody thing was pointing downwards. It was doing my head in...deep breaths...positive thoughts. Okay, I just accepted it and moved on. Onwards and upwards, or downwards as was the case. My fingers stuck rigidly to the string locations and I was strumming; nothing ground-breaking but hey man, I was playing the guitar. The book told me I was doing ever so well, so I thanked the book for the compliment and eagerly awaited the blow-job or even the next instruction. *Now try alternating downstrokes with upstrokes.* I duly obeyed and I strummed up and down, keeping my left fingers super-glued to the fret board in the D major position.

Eventually I managed to prize my fingers off the neck of the guitar and, like a man almost possessed, I moved onto the next chord: the A Major; he was another 'happy chappy' and apparently best mates with D Major. This was a bit more tricky than the D chord, as three of my fingers needed to fit onto one fret and having oversized phalanges, that was easier said than done. However, I adopted my tried and tested approach of placing each finger on the appropriate string one by one and eventually I was strumming up and down again. It was the same scenario for the E chord. I was having fun, limited maybe in its variety, but fun all the same.

At this juncture I should point out that while progression through lessons 1 to 6 was rapid, the task in Lesson 7 of learning 3 different chords was still challenging me, even after a couple of weeks. It was a painfully slow and humiliating process and one that probably infringed the human rights of all those within ear shot. As I tried to become more fluent in the spontaneity of my chord changes, I found that my fingers had created their own anarcho-syndicalist commune and at their bi-weekly meeting had decided to work independently of one another and rebel against the dictatorship of my cerebellum. I couldn't understand why this was happening as my fingers had always been most obedient when it had come to performing a steady rhythm!

I decided to move on and I encountered the minor chords. I was now presented with my first theory query; what the hell was the difference between a minor and major chord? Having completely ignored music at school (as well as most other subjects) I had no grasp of music theory. So I eagerly trawled through the book to be enlightened as to the Major, Minor question. Unfortunately, even though it was a beginner's book, it didn't cater for the pre-beginner, beginner. The one piece of information I could find was that the minor chord was a sad chord. I'd already learnt that the major chord was a happy chord, so I deduced that the happy/sad sound must be the difference. Crikey, I was starting to understand theory; I was on a high, but it soon dawned on me the real reason why they were called sad chords…I was depressed as fuck when I tried to learn them.

After another couple of weeks of musical GBH I could finally strum (sort of) the so called 'piss easy' chords of D minor, A minor and E minor. I had also progressed onto moving between the chords without a gap of three minutes to change chord position. My slow progress was frustrating and on many occasions my new guitar nearly joined my bullworker, exercise bike and *Learn French in 30 Days* CD up in the loft. Instead, I kept focussing on the potential groupie rewards and the guitar was spared retirement – but only just. It was clear that the whole guitar-playing malarkey was not going to come easy to me. But aged 37 and with a vision of a better place, this meant it was a challenge, as opposed to age 17 when, with no patience whatsoever, it meant *bollocks to that, I'm off to the pub.* This time I wasn't going to give in so easily.

At this stage in my life I'd become something of an expert on the principles of behavioural change, as not only was it a key part of my job, but I had also spent most of my adult life attempting it. I therefore knew, to a degree, what to do in order to tackle the inevitable feelings of pointlessness and hopelessness that occur when change doesn't happen as quickly as you'd like it to. In effect, I had become an expert on pointlessness and hopelessness.

One of the key principles was to have a good plan so I set about devising a foolproof, cast iron, 10-point plan.

- Objective 1: Be curious. I told myself that, at the very least, I wanted to know how much better I could be if I practised for six months.
- Objective 2: Not to set myself impossible practice targets. To do little and often and not worry about speed of progress, as long as there *was* some progress.
- Objective 3: To enrol for guitar lessons.
- Objective 4: To fire the guitar teacher if he/she tries to get me to learn a non-rock song.
- Objective 5: To set myself short term, reinforcing goals.
- Objective 6: Not to get pissed off when I don't achieve my short term reinforcing goals.
- Objective 7: To take time to continually remind myself that some of the best songs ever written were apparently easy and simple.
- Objective 8: To take time to continually delude myself.

- Objective 9: To take my guitar into the crapper with me, because that is apparently what Jimi Hendrix used to do.
- Objective 10: See objective 8.

Although my 'Easy Steps to Learning to Play the Guitar' book stated categorically that, in order to progress properly, it was essential to complete and master each exercise in order, I was getting a little tired and irritated at repeating major and minor chords and playing *Silent Night* (not to be confused with *Black Night*). I wasn't even bloody interested in chords. My ignorant mind had convinced itself that the guitar greats didn't bother with chords and left that shit job to the rhythm guitarist. No, I wanted to be a solo-shredding lead guitarist.

So I went out and bought the tuition book: *Lead Guitar for Beginners to Advanced Students.*

I figured that now I had my 10-point plan it wouldn't be long before I would reach advanced status so I saw this as an investment in the future as well as the present. I sat down with my guitar plugged in and my amp throbbing and turned to:

Lesson 1: Tuning Your Guitar. For crying-out-loud, not again. *Are all these books written by the same person or something?* I thought to myself. I quickly turned the page.

Lesson 2: Scales. I'd heard about scales, mainly whispers, tales around the campfire, that sort of thing. Stories about young music students found wandering around aimlessly, manically repeating 'Do, Re, Mi, Fa, So, La, Ti, Do'. Others so traumatised by scales that they disappeared mid-term, emerging many years later with bald heads and wearing an orange blanket. But this was just scaremongering, stories that had been exaggerated over the years. Surely scales couldn't be that bad? Of course they weren't, if you were willing to practise ten hours a day and had the capacity to absorb mind bogglingly boring repetition without getting homicidal. For the half hour a day 'practicer' like myself, scales seemed like some ancient code that would take more than my lifetime to crack. Soon I was back to the equally mind bogglingly boring, but at least achievable three chord strumming and occasionally the comfort of my trusty air guitar.

Chapter 6

Growing Up
(March 1973 – Age 11   '... there are two paths you can go by...')

In 1973 on a street in my home village of Hagley a wise man from Hayley Green who had long blond curly hair stopped in front of me. People seemed to know him but I had never seen him before. I told him I had a dream of living a different life; to find the real me. He asked me why I wanted to do this. I told him I didn't know. He asked me if I had a plan of how to achieve my dream. I said I didn't. He asked me if I would know when I had reached my destination. I said no. He asked me if my brain hurt. I looked at him blankly. He pondered. Then he pondered some more. My heart was pounding with the anticipation of his wisdom on how I could realise my dream. Then he put his hand on his chin, furrowed his brow and uttered the wise words:

"It makes me wonder.........if there's a bustle in your hedgerow, don't be alarmed now, it's just a spring clean for the May Queen. Yes there are two paths you can go by, but in the long run, there's still time to change the road you're on."

Wow, I was blown away. I closed my eyes, tilted my head backwards and breathed in the inspiration of his wisdom. Many seconds passed and then I opened my eyes and excitedly asked the wise man, "What the hell does that mean?" But he had gone, vanished.

Undeterred, I let this great wisdom germinate inside of me.

June 1973

A month before my 11-plus, a strange thing happened. We were all shepherded into the Junior School Sports Hall and were told that there was going to be a special demonstration for us. A make-shift screen had been erected so we couldn't guess what the nature of this demonstration was going to be. We all sat there in a state of excited anticipation and were generally glad to have our normal classroom routine interrupted. One of the teachers took the screen away and we were presented with a very young child sitting behind a drum kit. He was introduced, but none of us had heard of him or the famous group his father played in. His performance was mesmerising and I remember thinking how lucky he was to have been able to learn a skill that well at such a young age. There was a kind of freedom to the whole scenario and although the experience was anoetic, the event planted (deep, deep down) the first seeds of what would become my pursuit of a lifestyle outside of mainstream convention. The name of the drummer: Jason Bonham – aged at that time, 6 years and 11 months. Smart-arsed kid!

Chapter 7

Learning to Play the Guitar: Part 3
(1999: First Guitar Lesson – Age 37)

I needed help. I needed a guitar teacher. Or to use their other title…a struggling musician. I decided to go through a proper music academy and I was put in touch with a guitarist named John. Now at this point in my guitar playing career I had less confidence than a drop out who'd just lost his undisputed World's Biggest Loser title, so the last thing I wanted were for the lessons to be held in a venue where lots of people might be milling around. So off I trotted to the quiet seclusion of Mobberley Primary School(!), just outside Knutsford in Cheshire, to meet my guitar teacher. I parked in the school grounds and made my way past the hordes of kids and parents who were there for after school activities. As I looked for the classroom that John was in, I congratulated myself on another fine mess I'd gotten myself into. Eventually I located John and learnt that he was a 20-something Liverpudlian who played in a band and taught the guitar to children…and I was his only adult pupil.

Clearly the information I had given to the academy - that I was a beginner - had not filtered through to John who seemed highly energised by my arrival. He was obviously weary of the rigid format he had to adhere to when teaching children and was looking forward to interacting with a 'proper guitarist'. I was told to bring my own guitar and as I didn't have an acoustic, this meant rolling up with my *axe* in one hand and my amp in the other, which just added to the charade.

After the initial pleasantries John asked me what I wanted to learn. In retrospect the question was obviously meant to reference the impending lesson. However I went straight off on a tangent.

"Eruption by Van Halen." His eyes lit up like I'd just offered him a recording contract and he smiled enthusiastically, which produced a reciprocal reaction in me.

"Okay," he said "technically it's a tricky one, so give me an example of where you're at right now."

So I picked up my axe, plugged it in, turned the volume up to 11, pressed the distortion button and then carefully placed each finger, one by one on the guitar neck to make the A major chord; I then strummed the guitar and repeated the process for the D major and E major chords, creating the unforgettable sound of *Silent Night*. Then I looked up at John and smiled at him like Liberace. John had that look that you rarely see in a man, like he was witnessing something that was just too much to take in – his brain simply did not have a response to the stimuli he was being presented with. I now recognise that look to be one of shock. However, at the time I thought it was a look of pleasurable surprise at the impressive self-taught standard I had reached. After a short while John came to his senses, put a halt to my demonstration of guitar wizardry and with a heavy sigh he began the lesson.

I found guitar lessons an uncomfortable experience. Every time John gave me an instruction, even the most simple of instructions, my mind would crash and I would sit there doing my Captain Jerk impression. Totally gormless, not a flicker. I would just stare into space like someone had switched me off. It was just like 32 years ago when I started infant school. I couldn't decide whether it was my age, my complete lack of talent or my complete lack of confidence that was causing the problem. I mean, he was only showing me simple scale patterns. Luckily for me John was an extremely patient and understanding teacher and occasionally he would give me sound advice, like…"don't give up your day job you useless piece of shit."

John persevered and one week he thought it would be a good idea if I learnt some music theory. "Okay," I said "I'll give it a go, it can't be that difficult." After all, I'd already learnt the difference between major and minor chords and I was keen to learn more. Another big mistake. My guitar was in severe danger of trading places with my *Learn French in 30 Days* CD. It soon became apparent that music theory made no sense whatsoever. For a start, there are six strings on a guitar, but only five lines on the music sheet (something they call a Stave). Then you have eight notes in an octave but only the five lines to represent them on. So what ends up happening is that notes are written willy-nilly all over the place because there aren't enough lines on the sheet music to start with. To me, they just haven't thought it through.

The following is an extract from a music theory lesson that was for beginner guitarists:

The major scale of C is written on the stave without any accidentals at all. If you want to play the same scale starting – let us say – from G, then you find that the last four notes do not match. They should be two tones and a semitone but are instead a tone, a semitone and a tone (D-E-F-G). For that reason we must raise the F by a semitone, which gives us F sharp.

It would be easier to explain the rules of cricket to an American.

Je m'appelle Pierre – vous voudrez un guitar?

In mid-1999 a guitar magazine was advertised on TV called *Play Guitar*. It stated there would be fortnightly editions in which it would take the absolute beginner through a simple step-by-step guide to learning to play the guitar and learning simple but classic rock songs. I eagerly went and purchased the first edition. I waded through a bit of 'history of the guitar' crap and on page seven I noticed the heading, 'Reading Music Made Easy.' Then it said "People are sometimes put off learning to play an instrument by the appearance of written music." No shit! Of course people are put off. It makes no bloody sense. But there was more. The next heading was 'Tablature.' Now this sounded more like it, they said it's:

Easier to read than standard music notation because it's designed specifically for the guitar. Although it's sometimes thought of as less 'highbrow' than standard notation.

Oh, excuse me if us non-music reading plebs have to resort to some lazy-persons-guide to reading music. But there was still more. Apparently TAB (as it's called by the guitar playing proletariat) is actually a very old system and in fact the first written *axe* music was in this form. Well blow me, seems like the 'Tablaturists' must have been driven out by the 'Notationalists.' I can see it now:

Centuries ago anti-Tablature propaganda was produced and the followers of such writings were ostracised and driven underground by the establishment - the 'Notationalists.' Those caught were subjected to 'Notationalist' torture…locked in a room and made to listen to hours and hours of crotchets and quavers. Most cracked and were forced to follow the 'Notationalists' scriptures; a few held out, but were reduced to broken men when the much feared demi-semiquavers were brought out. Interestingly, some of the old followers of the faith like 'Leonardo De Axeman' made secret references to Tablature in their songs. Recently, old TABs have been found hidden under Roslyn Chapel in Scotland and now a whole new generation of 'Tablaturists' can be seen whipping themselves on their backs with old E-strings as they try and learn Stairway to Heaven.

So TAB was my route into reading music. What was great about TAB was that it had six lines on the paper like the six strings on the guitar. Although they did throw in the odd curve ball in terms of that on the guitar the bass (i.e. the thickest) string is at the top. Yet the top line of the TAB relates to the notes of the bottom

(E) string...the thinnest string. This pissed me right off and made my brain ache. But anyway, apart from that and one other small point that I will touch on later, it was good for non-music reading beginners. The notes appeared as numbers, so even a total 'rocking amoeba' like myself could grasp the concept. Yep, I was excited.

I'd now been practicing for a couple of months and by this stage a few chords were starting to sound like, well, chords. Still slow and tortured, but chords nevertheless and I could make sense of some theory. What I needed now was a scale that was piss-easy; cue the pentatonic scale (surely the scale of choice for the Death Metal boys). For musical donkeys like me the pentatonic scale was a gift from the musical Gods. A simple five note scale that apparently all the rock greats used and one that BB King had made a whole career out of. Now surely this was within my capabilities? The answer was a big fat NO.

As a concept isolated from the goal of creating a pleasant musical experience for the ear, the scale was a most splendid musical innovation, but in terms of the simple act of learning five notes and off you go supporting BB King on his next world tour, it was a long way from achieving that objective. You see the problem lay in the timing. What quickly became apparent as I eagerly reproduced the notes to my favourite guitar solo in the strict 'tab' order was it sounded nothing bloody like it. In fact, it sounded more like the pentatonic scale I had been practising, but in a different note order. Yes, it became clear there was a fundamental flaw in the concept of TAB. The flaw being it gave me no indication of how much time there needed to be between notes. I'm not going to go too much into musical theory because, as I'm sure you've gathered by now, I know sod all about it; but what I did learn, and excuse me for blinding you with science, was that if you don't know how much time there needs to be between notes, you're fucked.

So to recap, with TAB I knew which notes to play but I didn't know how quickly or slowly to play them. So what was the answer? Friggin' notation - there was no getting away from it. It was back to those quavers, crotchets and bloody demisemiquavers. Bollocks!

My first six months were up and I had played my 'curiosity card' (objective 1 of my plan). Yes there had been some progress, slow progress, but some progress all the same. After a similar period of time, I'm sure some smart-arsed kid would have already been *duck-walking* his way through *Eruption*, but for me it was still a matter of mastering the basics. Having some knowledge of the principles of skill acquisition, I was aware that the slowest progress was always at the start and momentum can build up quickly once the basics are in place. I figured that if I kept it going then anything was possible. I kept telling myself that one thing was for sure; if I gave in, I would always be left wondering what came after the demisemiquaver(*), so I had to keep going. And besides, all I had experienced so far was a combination of frustration, desperation, humiliation and constipation. I hadn't had any fun yet, like booking into rehab, so I extended my six-month curiosity-card into a five-year goal.

(* it's the hemidemisemiquaver)

Chapter 8

The Gig Scene
(1976 Continued)

Hawkwind - 16th Sept 1976
(Birmingham Odeon, £2.00, Front Stalls, D5).

To me, Hawkwind were *a rock riddle, wrapped in a progressive mystery, inside a psychedelic enigma.* We had stories of theatrical stage shows – almost Pythonesque in their content. We had Lemmy, a man who could supposedly consume any alcoholic concoction known to man and still talk to you as if he'd had half a bitter shandy. And then we had Silver Machine, a 1972 chart hit, which in our eyes - as we couldn't afford albums - represented Hawkwind's complete repertoire. To an inquisitive 14 year old this band had to be investigated.

Talking of Lemmy, wouldn't it have been great for a supergroup to have formed with Lemmy on bass; John Bonham on drums; Bon Scott on vocals and on guitar,

Slash (in his drinking days). A hell-raising cocktail that surely would have exploded and then imploded in seconds. But boy, what expectation would have come with that line-up. It would have been like putting Ali, Frasier, Foreman and Tyson into the ring simultaneously, ringing the bell and then running for cover as you waited for the atom to split. But I digress.

Back at the Hawkwind gig, the demographic of the audience seemed different. We arrived at the Odeon at about seven o'clock - we always liked to arrive early to take in the atmosphere and make sure we didn't miss the support band. Hawkwind's support band was Tiger who were great and during the break we waxed lyrical about the big lead guitarist. But it had seemed that half the crowd couldn't be bothered to watch them and those that did had been intent on giving them a hard time. The crowd had felt different to the Rainbow crowd – older, more cynical and during the gig we felt our (young) age. When Tiger's set came to an end they received 'enthusiastic' applause, but I wasn't sure if it was ironic or heartfelt. Personally, I was like a sponge, absorbing all aspects of rock music, support bands and all, and I was *sure* I would never become so blinkered.

Hawkwind were amazing. Not just from a musical point of view but from the perspective of the whole package.

The lead singer was bizarre to the extreme, making more costume changes than you would see at a Danny La Rue impersonator convention. From an Arabian Knight to a gas mask.

At one point we weren't sure what he was wearing, as someone must have turned the dry-ice machine up to eleven. I'd never seen so much fog at a gig before. In fact, for a while that is *all* we could see and when it sounded like the start of *Silver Machine* we all stood up and manically started running in all directions. When we got to what we hoped was the front there was zero percent visibility, so we all looked around to check we hadn't accidentally ended up in the toilet. Strange, when you think about it. We ran to the front to get a better view but we couldn't see a thing.

I nudged Huw.

"Can you see anything?" I asked.

"What?" Huw said in a husky voice which I put down to him breathing in too much dry ice.

"I said, can you see anything?"

"Who the fuck are you?" I no longer put 'Huw's' strange voice down to the dry ice!

As the fog gradually cleared I could just make out that the lads were to the right of the rock-head who had so politely enquired as to my identity. Seeing as he looked like he was auditioning for a part in 'Vampire Bikers from Hell,' I quickly made my way over to the lads.

"Look." Huw said, pointing at the stage.

I looked. "What is it?"

Huw pondered. "Looks like a load of lights shining out of what appears to be…appears to be…a chemistry set."

Spinal Tap was eight years away. And although many bands have claimed to be the influence behind Spinal Tap – Saxon being the favourites – Hawkwind must have had some creative input. From above the stage appeared what looked like a kind of Heath Robinson designed pastiche of atoms, crystals and lots of glass from which emanated a host of strange colours. Was it meant to represent Stonehenge? Had the creative designer eaten the wrong type of mushroom? Who knows?

I thought I recognised one of the tracks, but I couldn't be sure, most of the stuff they played seemed to be new material. But the visual stuff and the dry ice kept us entertained - obviously not at the same time. It was pure theatre but no one had a clue what the plot was about. Maybe Hawkwind didn't know either? But at the end of the day no one really cared. They were just great fun. Slightly bonkers, but great fun all the same.

Silver Machine never materialised although we all cheered loudly when one of the band members appeared in a spacesuit but they were just teasing us.

The encore meant we left the gig as happy rockers as it was their version of Steppenwolf's classic, *Born to be Wild*.

A few days later I read a review of the gig and realised that our excitement at seeing Lemmy had been misplaced. Apparently, he had been kicked out of the band after spending five days in a Canadian prison for (alleged) drug possession. The fact that I had not noticed this, having stood only 20 feet (length) by 8 feet (height) away from Lemmy's replacement...the bass player Paul Rudolph, I blamed on the dry ice. Not sure I got away with it though!

Review from the Birmingham Evening Mail

Too much noise

Hawkwind, Odeon, Birmingham

TAKE AWAY Hawkwind's pain-producing amplification, the strobes, the pretty lights, the man with the gas mask, the Rudolph Valentino singer and some hammy theatricals and there's not a lot left.

They're a band who seem to have got trapped in a strange psychedelic time warp but they seem to have a lot of fans.

I'm not one of them and felt their immense noise did nothing more than stop me enjoying the lights.

On the other hand the support, Tiger, know all about enjoyment. With Big Jim Sullivan on guitar, they have the enthusiasm and good musical ideas to market.

They had a hard job cutting through the anticipation but managed it confidently.

With numbers like "Blue Space" which took Sullivan's stunning guitar work and combined it with some gentle digs at today's pop, their forthcoming LP should be a winner.

SANDY COUTTS

Thin Lizzy - 26th Oct 1976

(Birmingham Odeon, £1.80, Rear Stalls, BB3)

Huw and Steve were sitting either side of me. We had just watched the support band Clover and the venue was filling up as the support band-boycotting majority made their way to their seats. As usual the atmosphere was starting to build.

"Go on…now…go on," I wasn't sure whether Huw was encouraging or goading me.

"Yeah, we'll join in as soon as you start it up," Steve stoked up the fire.

I anxiously surveyed the crowd; there were hundreds of rockers in view.

"Why don't you shout it out?" I voiced the question to Steve, but quickly moved my head to my left to indicate that the question was applicable to Huw as well.

"Let's shout it out together." Huw's suggestion had merit.

"Okay, but we better hurry otherwise we'll be beaten to it," I said, totally oblivious to the sad level of gravitas I was displaying.

Steve picked up on the need for quick united action "Right, after three – are we all in?"

"Let's do it!" shouted Huw.

Steve started the count "One, two, three!"

"WALLY!"

The pre-concert build up had invariably involved a multitude of 'Wally' cries and up to this point we had been sheep-like followers of this cry. But with over six month's concert going experience under our belts, we had felt it was our time to rouse the gaggle into a frenzy of excitement. Now we could sit back and admire our handy work as the pack took the bait and responded with *Wally* cries all over the venue.

Why were we continually shouting for Wally? One theory is that a roadie named Wally went missing at a gig and as the crowd were taking their seats his name was being called out over the main mic. This was like a red rag to a bull to the highly excitable minds of the rock crowd and one bright spark decided to aid the search with his own cries. This of course resulted in a sheep-like frenzy of shouts for the missing Wally. No one is sure if he was ever found but, just to be on the safe side future rock crowds always took it upon themselves to check if Wally was anywhere to be seen.

The innovative mind of the rocker would soon start to tire of the Wally cry and in 1979, the Life of Brian influenced "Albatross" shout started up and for a number of concerts (after this), both Wally and

82

Albatross were vying for first place on the 'shoutometer'. This sartorial shouting was eventually taken to new heights when one Darwinian town-crier shouted 'Heinz Baked Beans' but this level of innovation was far too abstract for the majority of us and this cry would usually be followed by general shaking of heads and the dismissive utterances of "tosser."

Old habits die hard and at a Classical Spectacular concert I attended many years later (yes, rockers can be cultured), I completely forgot where I was and suddenly found myself standing up and shouting out *Wally* (okay, we're not that cultured). I heard a couple of the 'classical-heads' say "what a strange person", while most of them just stared at me with a confused look on their faces. However, one member of the crowd with long grey hair turned round and uttered the beautiful affirmation "Yes?" In over 20 years of concert going, no one had ever said 'yes' to the *Wally* cry. My search was over, obviously the mysterious roadie had done a runner and switched musical genres; no wonder we could never find him.

Back at the Thin Lizzy concert, the Wally cries continued until the lights went down and then the shouts turned to cheers as Phil Lynott and the boys took to the stage.

Post Lizzy gig we were walking to the station on yet another rock concert high.

"That was up there with Rainbow!" As 'experienced' rockers, all gigs were now being compared to our benchmark favourites.

"Yeah, it was a no-nonsense proper rock gig," Steve added to my opening gambit with an equally enthusiastic tone. We had now started to try and impress each other with our *subtle* and *insightful* nuances of the rock scene.

"I know what you mean, they're just...just rock, hard rock... you know what I mean?" I got the feeling they didn't. "And their lyrics have meaning...you know...about lads and women and stuff...sort of proper rock songs...you know what I mean?" I was sure they didn't. "What shall we do tomorrow?"

I was very intense about rock. Yes, I could take the piss out of it, but deep down it meant everything to me and it was one of the few subjects that I would offer any personal insights or philosophies on. The only information that stuck in my brain was rock related; all other topics just didn't seem to make it into my long-term memory. Yes, I did have opinions and thoughts on other subjects but I kept those strictly to myself. So I started to build my whole self-concept around rock. When I did try to offer my opinion on a subject (and as I say, this was usually around the rock scene) then I liked to adopt the smash and grab style of philosophising. That is, I would say my bit and then quickly change the subject before anyone had the chance to pull it apart and make me look like a rock loser – or at very least I hoped everyone just agreed with it.

Unfortunately, on this occasion Huw ignored my attempt to change the subject and returned to the debate "Yeah, they're like a heavier version of Quo." Blimey, I thought, he seemed to be agreeing with me. This was a great relief as I had no empirical evidence to back up my hypothesis.

"Don't be a knob," Steve replied to Huw's remark. "Quo aren't a rock band."

I was relieved that the pressure was on Huw and having gained some confidence from Huw's apparent affirmation of my theory, I picked up on Steve's comment and waded in with a fresh dose of bullshit.

"Yeah, Zeppelin are rock, they're like...true rock and Sabbath, they're, they're...heavy rock and Purple, they're like er, loud rock, and..." I'd forgotten what I was trying to say.

"Lizzy?" prompted Huw.

"Yes, that was it Lizzy...Lizzy are like...they're like, kind of street rock...whereas Quo, they're like...they're like.....like three chord rock...you know what I mean?" I was suddenly awash with debating confidence and was pretty pleased with my critique of the whole rock genre. The depth of my critical faculties had completely floored the lads as there was total silence. More tumbleweed to add to my ever growing stock pile.

Eventually Huw replied by saying "I know that, but what are you trying to say?" It was one of those statements that we used now and again to indicate that the recipient of the statement was talking out of his arse or starting to think what he had to say was important or interesting. It was a statement that you knew there was no point in replying to, as it would be continually repeated until you realised that you were indeed talking out of your arse. Deep down I was relieved, as it meant the debate was over.

The subject quickly turned to how we had now graduated to perceived rock-concert going legends, because we had started the first Wally cry. And our egos hadn't even had their 15th birthdays!

Review from the Birmingham Evening Mail

The new Rock superstars

Odeon, New Street, Birmingham

THIN LIZZY seem destined to be Britain's latest Rock superstars.

Not only were they acclaimed as such by last night's ecstatic audience, they also look the part.

Most importantly they play superb, gutsy, aggressive music with verve and style.

The last British rock band to have such a devastating effect on audiences were Status Quo, who until now have been unrivalled in the field of out-and-out rock.

But Thin Lizzy may knock even Status Quo from their perch.

Last night they delivered an electrifying pounding performance which few bands could live with.

Such songs as "Rosalie" and "The Warrior" have helped raise Thin Lizzy from the also-rans to the front-runners.

Phil Lynott is an excellent singer/bassist, but it is the power and aggression of twin lead guitarists Brian Robertson and Scott Graham which makes Thin Lizzy one of the tightest, most entertaining and enjoyable bands in Britain.

KEN LAWRENCE.

ONCERT

Gallagher

support

L, BIRMINGHAM

December, 1976

3160

Rory Gallagher - 18th Dec 1976

(Old Bingley Hall)

We had now all turned 15 and we had already established almost a year of concert going experience. Other lads from the local area, who were our age and into rock, were just starting to gain the parental freedom or rock *nouse* to access the gig sub-culture. In a nutshell, when it came to the rock scene, we really did think we were 'cool.'

It was roughly this time that the local party circuit started to enter our radar and as we considered ourselves an integral part of the scene it seemed a given that for the party to be a success we had to be invited. Our self-delusion was taken to new heights when after the Rory Gallagher gig (Saturday 18th December 1976) we went to a local house party. We arrived carrying a couple of warm cans of Colt 45 malt liquor (between us!) and Julie the party host greeted us at the door, wondering who was trying to crash her party two hours after everyone else had arrived. When she recognised us, she welcomed us in and the sound of rock music was emanating from the lounge. We

88

rolled in proudly displaying our Rory Gallagher rock concert medals and we were soon eulogising about the gig with the articulation skills of Chewbacca the Wookiee.

"Man, he was on fire, we were there right next to this huge stack of amps...there in front of us...you could see everything, everyone was just going mental. He was just awesome," I said with as much controlled composure as I could control.

A *chick* piped in (*chick* was one of the many endearing terms that we used {back then} as a reference to girls. For some reason the chicks referred to us as bankers or at least that's what it sounded like.) "How could you see if there was a stack of amps in front of you?"

Such attention to detail was, to say the least, slightly irritating and my reply should have been a short, swift *'the stage was to the left of the stack'*. But because she was a girl and I was a boy and she wasn't a dog and I was alert and desperate, I went for the sympathetic and understanding reply. "Would you like me to take you to a concert so you can find out?" When she walked off without even so much as a reply, the lads cried with laughter and after a short period trying to save face I joined them.

It was that period in life when everything seemed perfect – no responsibilities, a bit of money from part-time jobs and I was with a great bunch of lads. True, none of us had a girlfriend or the necessary chat up lines to get one, but it wouldn't be long before the oldest of our group, Steve, broke our collective duck.

Chapter 9

Learning to Play the Guitar: Part 4
(Months 6 – 12; Age 38)

The Sacred Guitar Solo

I decided to learn a proper rock song. Not *Silent Night*
or the usual songs that appear in the beginner books,
but a bona-fide, full-on, ball-breaking rock song. I was
in a newsagent and I noticed one of the guitar
magazines had a free CD with it, with backing tracks
and TABs to some of the 'all time rock classics',
including *Lazy* by Deep Purple. I love *Lazy*; it features
some of the best guitar work ever, so it seemed like a
good place to start. Wrong, wrong and treble friggin'
wrong. Talk about difficult. It wasn't long before I'd
eaten the TAB and was reduced to playing *Lazy* with
my air guitar. I needed to re-evaluate the criteria I used
for my song selection. After much thought I decided I
needed a rock song that was easy to play. Cue *All
Right Now*. This was the business. I was finally up and
running and although my picking was a bit ham-fisted
and my fretting was as subtle as Motorhead playing at
a Women's Institute's afternoon tea party, I was
starting to learn songs that for years had seemed like
the preserve of a different race. This is an important
point to make. When you have listened to rock songs
and guitar solos for years and years and many of the
songs have become emotionally and spiritually

entwined with your very being, then the songs take on a kind of God-like quality. Like something you believe in, but you will never touch or truly understand. For non-guitar playing followers of the faith, all we could do was to worship with our air guitars and be not-worthy of the musical gifts our rock gods were giving us. This is one thing people who learn rock guitar from a young age will never appreciate. A classic guitar solo is much more than just a guitar solo, it is sacred and for me to be playing those solos felt like a combination of exhilaration and sacrilege. Exhilaration because I was achieving something that I never thought would be possible; and sacrilege because I was completely annihilating them.

Guitar Style: 1999/2000

I once heard Carlos Santana state that every note you play should have its own emotion and character. That a note is more than just a note; it's not just to be played as a process in a technical exercise, but it is the representation of the feeling within a melody or song. That, of course, is pure twaddle to a guitar playing donkey like myself. But I kind of understand what he means. There are clearly many excellent professional guitar players that have a technical mastery that is unbelievable but, alas, they lack the necessary feel to go with it.

I read that Richie Sambora adopts the 'less is more' principle in his guitar work, which means that Richie has something in common with me; as my guitar work is based on the 'less is the only option' style of guitar playing. Of course, that is not to say I wouldn't mind reaching the 'why use one note in a beat when you can use ten' standard, but it's a talent thing, or lack of it, that is holding me back.

Fast guitar playing is also referred to as shredding. Shredding is the complete antithesis of the 'every note is sacred' style. It's fast, it's furious and boy, does it look good. A guaranteed totty recruiting exercise if you can pull it off. Alas, if you have aspirations to shred, but no talent to match, it can all go horribly wrong and, dare I say it, sound like a bloody racket. As Clint once said, 'a man must know his limitations', and in music that phrase especially holds true. It's better to do an easy song well than a hard song badly. That may sound obvious, but I believe I'm not the only one who has tried far too early to play at a level way above one's capabilities. Some days you can't help yourself; you have to let rip and start shredding on all cylinders, man and guitar in perfect disharmony. In reality the only shredding that I will ever do well at is at work and of the paper variety, but that's such a shit pun that I think I'll phone the Samaritans.

****

Also, as you will read later, I have a different slant on the 'it's better to do an easy song well than a hard song badly' maxim.

Chapter 10

Growing Up

(1973 – First Year at the Grange Comprehensive School. Age 11)

I failed my 11-plus exam which came as no surprise to me as I hadn't really fully engaged in the statutory diktat of enlightening oneself in the core subjects of reading, writing and arithmetic. For my insolence I was given 5 years at the Grange Comprehensive School, Lye, near Stourbridge (now the Pedmore High School).

The Grange was a rough secondary school, with many of the kids hardened from having started life at the back of the grid. It was a difficult environment and what made things worse was that the core base of my security blanket - my friends, including Huw, had all confidently marched off to Grammar school.

Chapter 11

Learning to Play the Guitar: Part 5
(Years 1 – 2; Age 39)

A New Guitar (Jan 2000)

It seems an integral part of the guitarist sub-culture is to own about 10 guitars. It doesn't matter if it means re-mortgaging the house; it just has to be done.

Now I'd been hacking away at my Squire beginner's Strat for about a year and I thought it was about time that I purchased the obligatory second guitar. I was living in Sunbury-on-Thames, so I made the trip round the M25 to Anderton's music store in Guildford.

I'm a bit of a sceptic when it comes to more expensively priced goods, as I think most of the time you're paying for the name and not extra quality. So when I eventually got past the Goths, I sidled up to the aspiring/failed rock guitarist sales assistant and said:

"Do the more expensive guitars actually sound any better than the cheaper crap you have on sale?" In hindsight I could have worded it a bit better, as my question was followed by one of those long 'what the fuck do we have here' silences. Eventually he smiled, although it could have been a grimace, and spoke through clenched teeth.

"Yes, sir, a much better sound." For the first time in my life I was suddenly able to read a person's thought bubble. It read:

'20 years I've been playing the guitar and look what my life has come to, serving dip-shits like this. Where did it all go wrong?'

Although I'd always wanted to own a Gibson Les Paul Custom, I'd got used to the feel and sound of my Squire Strat, so I picked out a factory made Fender Stratocaster for consideration. It was about £400 so a decent step upwards in terms of cost. Basically the reason why more expensive guitars sound better is because they are made of more expensive solid woods like rosewood and mahogany and they are finished to a higher standard. And there will be differences in the quality grades for tuners, bridges, pickups, pick guards and tremolo mechanisms. I couldn't tell the difference, but I didn't let on. The guitar looked great and to be honest if I could, I'd have said, 'that will do nicely' and walked out without even trying the bugger. But it's a kind of unwritten rule in guitar shops that (unless you are buying a pre-boxed beginner's set) you must try out the axe to make sure it suits your style. This would have been fine if I actually had a style. My saving grace was that the shop had glass panelled sound proof rooms, so I could go in and try out the axe without any embarrassment. Alas, as I was soon to discover, a more expensive guitar didn't come with a guarantee promising a step upwards in terms of playing ability.

I entered the cubical, plugged the thing in and gave a nervous wave to my *friendly* shop assistant. I strummed merrily away at the chords I had learnt and they sounded marginally better than I was used to hearing on my old guitar, but that could have been down to a better amp. After a few minutes of strumming, the sales assistant was still staring intently into my booth, as if the whole thing was about to disappear like the TARDIS. So I thought I'd better do something more visual than slow strumming, so I started on my inimitable shredding technique which, in a sound proof booth, is the only place I can get away with it. Both my hands were going like the clappers. Unfortunately no coherent sound was being created; it was a right racket. When I came out of the booth, I was covered in about the same amount of sweat that I had secreted last time I emerged from a booth…in Amsterdam. Only this time I used the tissues to wipe my brow. Note to myself…*edit that bit out.* Note to author from reader…*you forgot you cranky old codger.*

Anyway, to cut a long story short I purchased the Fender Stratocaster and I was now the proud owner of two guitars. Other than that, buying a guitar is like marriage. The build-up is great, the moment of exchange is very emotional and it's a buzz for a few weeks afterwards. Unfortunately the realisation quickly dawns that in reality, nothing has changed. The routine is still the same and the only thing you're left with after the big day is a whopping great hole in your bank balance.

That night I went out with a few friends to watch a pub band and by the end of the evening I had categorically decided to return my new guitar back to the shop and stop chasing my stupid, stupid dream. I just didn't get it. How could such a great guitarist be playing in some flea-pit pub like that? It was mind boggling. So it was time for me to wise up, to face the truth, to stop following some silly middle-aged(ish) notion that I might become a rock guitarist. What had I been thinking? How could I have deluded myself so easily? There was no point in hiding behind empty visions of a place that didn't exist; from there on in, it was going to be an unfulfilling job, stress, school runs, dinner parties, annual holidays, divorce and membership of Fathers for Justice for me.

Of course that wasn't the first time I'd decided to give up my guitar playing aspirations. It had happened every time I'd gone out to watch a pub band, but the next day I would always pick up my axe and continue on my painful journey. Musicianship allows you incredible scope in the art of rationalisation. When you think about it, some of the best musicians in the world have never achieved mainstream success and yet some of the most average musicians have. I mean, if I was the quickest 100m runner in the world, I wouldn't be turning up at club meetings with half a dozen people in attendance watching in amazement at my running speed. I would be on the world stage. Yet an amazingly talented musician can regularly turn up at a small pub and put on a world shattering performance. So every time it happens, the next morning I pick up my guitar and remind myself that in the music industry, it's much more about feel than ability – more about delusion than reality. Then the dream is back on.

One day I decided that I needed to build up my confidence of playing in front of people. I was aware of a pub near where I was living, which was now in Matlock, Derbyshire. The pub was called The

Fishpond, and they had an acoustic open mic night on Sunday evenings. Okay, there was a slight technical hitch in as much as I didn't own an acoustic guitar and I wasn't that interested in the unplugged side of things. But I figured I needed to boost my confidence and a quick strum in front of half a dozen like-minded pissed up people sounded perfect. So I borrowed an acoustic guitar for the evening, picked out a couple of well-known songs (from my *vast* repertoire) and headed on down.

Chapter 12

Growing Up
(June 1975: The Rock Connection. Age 13)

I hadn't a clue why I was here and no one was offering me any clues. I never had any aspirations to be anything; not a doctor, sportsman, musician, plumber, train driver or astronaut. I did feel a big passion for something - I just hadn't a clue what it was. Then music entered my world.

Very rarely were album-only groups like Sabbath and Zeppelin played on the radio, and because I wasn't exposed to them it was hard to embrace those sounds. There was a huge monopoly and oligopoly when it came to music and kids like me were brainwashed with so called commercially appealing pop through the chart obsessed outlets of Radio 1 and Top of the Pops. Radio 2 was for the parents and there was no satellite TV. Radio Luxemburg used to play the odd variation from the norm, but really the only way to engage with alternative sounds was through the dodgy and constantly changing reception of Radio Caroline. Unlike today where kids can pick and choose their musical tastes from a young age, we had to wait for changes in social norms, advances in communication, or for the musical wisdom to be passed on.

At this point in my life, June 1975, I was thirteen and starting to become aware of a sound that seemed to make more of a connection with my soul. The energy that groups like Slade and Sweet generated excited my immature and barely developed auditory receptors, but it still didn't feel quite *right*. Something was missing. I needed an intervention that would speed up the maturation of my hearing organs – I needed the OBS (Older Brother Syndrome).

It was a bright summer's day in late June, 1975 and I was on the landing minding my own business, when Malc's door suddenly opened and he grabbed me by the arm and bundled me into his room. (My mum and dad had 3 sons. I'm the youngest, Malc is next and Greg is the oldest or Greg the Elder as he likes to be called when he's in the sauna with his friends).

"Meet me in the garage in 5 minutes," Malc whispered.

Before I had time to give him my intended - *you must be kidding, do you think I'm stupid or something?* - retort, he was off running down the stairs to the garage. This left me with a dilemma. Should I desist from walking into what I perceived to be a certain trap or should I follow my intense feelings of curiosity? I decided on the latter option.

As I entered the garage I saw Malc sitting in our parents' white Austin Princess. He pointed for me to sit in the passenger seat. Any lingering suspicions of a trap had now disappeared and I was now *really* curious. His eyes glanced up at the garage door, just to check that the coast was clear and from inside his coat pocket he got out a cassette tape and raised it in the air like it was the holy grail.

"Listen to this, it's awesome," he said with sermon-like authority and inserted the tape into the cassette player.

The first track started; keyboard – I scratched my brow, mmmmm - sounded like a church organ – he'd found religion! The tone of the keyboard made me drift into a really relaxed state and, what turned out to be the last note of the introduction, seemed to last forever. The note was fading off the edge of the universe and I was just about to board the good ship Zen, when the drums came in and scared me shitless. Then bang - guitar and bang – vocals. The track was *Speed King* by Deep Purple from their 1970 album 'Deep Purple in Rock.'

The hairs on the back of my neck freaked out and every sinew in my body seemed to awake from a thirteen year coma. The energy, the heavy sound, it was amazing. My rock DNA was on fire!

Malc stopped the tape.

"Well?" He was a man of few words.

"Bloody hell." I was a boy of limited descriptive qualities.

I pressed play. *Bloodsucker* followed *Speed King* and then…*Child in Time*. If *Speed King* had been an eye opener, then *Child in Time* was a full-on 'yank your eyes from their sockets' moment - just earth shattering. Having been fed on the safe Radio 1 'three minute' diet - songs with all the right nutrients, but ultimately, to me, totally indigestible, I was now in a parallel gastronomic universe. *Child in Time* was more than ten wonderful minutes long and as well as mind blowing guitar, there was a mind blowing 'scream out loud' vocal. If music be the food of love then I had just had a gigantic plate full of heart moving passion. By the end of the tape I felt as if I'd been in a time capsule that had taken me on a hypersonic journey of self-discovery. Now I had landed and as I got out of the car I felt a bit unsteady on my feet. I was in a state of shock. Suddenly I had found the key to unlock the angst I had been so carefully collecting for all those years. It felt invigorating and it felt scary. Rock music had entered me like a spirit and formed a perfect connection with my DNA. Deep down inside I knew I would embrace this feeling with all my heart. And never let it go.

Chapter 13

Learning to Play the Guitar: Part 6
(Winter 2000)

Apart from going to see a pub band, there's another sure fire way to completely shatter an aspiring guitarist's confidence and that is to go to an open mic night. Lots of pubs stage them, where any standard guitarist can get up and play a few numbers. Now when I heard about the open mic night, the 'any standard guitarist' phrase was the main selling point for me. I reasoned that I'd been playing for almost two years, so I must be better than some of the guitar hooligans they probably attracted. This assumption was to be added to my ever increasing catalogue of misguided assumptions I'd made since taking up the six string.

It's difficult to arrive incognito, do a reconnaissance and then decide if you want to play or not, because in order to play you have to bring along a bloody great big acoustic guitar. This is hard to hide when you walk through the door. What happens is that you arrive and your name is put down on a list and then you all sit round in a circle and one-by-one people play and sing. Some perform cover songs and some play their own compositions.

On this particular evening, by the time the third guitarist's stint had finished I'd already decided that humiliation on a scale hitherto unheard of for any human-being was about to befall me. The standard of guitar playing was staggering and they could all sing as well.

There was this one guy…it had come round to his turn. And he said, *this is a song I wrote on the way here*.

I thought *please, you must be having a laugh*. And then…I couldn't help myself. Before I knew it I'd said:

"Did you travel here from Australia?"

I was pretty pleased with my quick wit. But when silence ensued amongst the whole group an odd thought came into my head in terms of wondering where I was going to store all this bloody tumbleweed.

Anyway, he carried on. And to be fair his song was pretty good.

I was tempted to say, when it came round to my turn that *this is one I wrote in the toilet*, but as I didn't have any of my own songs I managed to stop myself. Instead, panic started to consume me and my mind entered 'flight' mode and I considered taking another piss break, doing a runner and sacrificing the stupid acoustic guitar. However as I had borrowed the guitar I figured this wasn't such a good idea, so I took a large swig out of my bottle of Newcastle Brown.

When I looked down at my play list, things got worse for my rapidly evaporating confidence: *Silent Night* in Chords A, D and E; and *When the Saints Go Marching In* in Chords…A, D and E. I was fucked; there was no two ways about it. This was my brother's fault. He was the one who had told me about the open mic night and it was his acoustic guitar I'd borrowed. What could I do? It would be my turn next; straight after 'Mr Guitar' who was in the process of finger picking his way through chord changes that simply weren't fair. As I looked at his face (he didn't even need to look at his guitar while playing) I couldn't help but think how I was going to shove his stupid guitar right up his smug arse if he didn't stop showing off before my go. And then I heard a voice:

"And we would like to welcome Pete to tonight's open mic. This is Pete's first time at the session, so give him a great round of applause."

All eyes turned on me. I picked up my guitar. I apologised to Lynyrd Skynyrd for what I was about to do and went straight into *Sweet Home Alabama*, followed later in the evening by *Feel Like Makin' Love*, by Bad Company. Yes, I did have a couple of other songs in my play list. But to be honest, I should have stuck to Silent Night because both the songs I played were way above my skill level. But I just couldn't resist it; I had to give them a go. I ignored the advice that every music book and music teacher gives you (the maxim I mentioned earlier on): *it's better to play the simple stuff well, than the difficult stuff badly.* Instead I turned it on its head by reasoning that *it's better to play a difficult song badly, than play an easy song badly.* And in any case by the time all the other guitarists had joined in with me i.e. come to my rescue (which I soon realised was the protocol at these acoustic nights) no one could hear that I was playing all the wrong notes in all the wrong order. Oh yes, I was having fun.

Chapter 14

Rock Music on the Radio

Immediately rock music became an obsession. The meaning in my life. I would eat, breathe and sleep rock music. I would listen to the radio as much as possible and discovered The Alan 'Fluff' Freeman Rock Show on Radio 1. It was on Saturday afternoons (from 1973 to 1978). That was pretty much the only avenue open that would lead you to all the old and new rock music. It was compelling listening. Saturday afternoons became such a wonderful time of musical discovery.

Tommy Vance then took over where 'Fluff' Freeman left off and he became one of the few music broadcasters in the United Kingdom to champion hard rock and heavy metal, providing the only national radio forum for both bands and fans. His Friday Rock Show became legendary amongst rock fans of that era.

And then there was John Peel. Yes, he was a bit hit and miss, but he did occasionally throw in some tasty treats.

And in the West Midlands a local rock radio presenter by the name of Robin Valk became a living legend amongst music fans with his rock show on BRMB radio that was broadcast towards the end of the 1970s.

In addition to the radio there was the print media. I would often queue outside the newsagents with the pensioners to get the first copy of Sounds and NME.

107

Although, the bloody pensioners would always push in.

There soon became a point when any track that had a decent guitar solo in, or sounded heavy, or was in the music press rock charts or, or, or … I would note down, with a view to at some point in the future (when I was old enough and had some money and knew where there was a good record shop) searching out an album by the band.

Now we have the digital era with specialist radio stations in the UK catering for all musical tastes. And of course, there is the Internet with music on tap. It's a different world. And I'm sure it's great, but in some ways it's sad that the excitement and the discovery has gone out of the experience.

Why Such A Connection? Part 1

DNA is the building block of life, so for me to have developed my rock DNA there must have been some hereditary connection. To validate this adolescent theory of mine I researched our family tree and what I found out sent me cold. I couldn't believe it. Apparently a great, grandmother on my mother's side went missing in the eighteen hundreds and no one ever found out what happened to her. The only information that was written about her was that she had dabbled in witchcraft whilst searching for the elixir of life. Apparently she had become a recluse and lived in a mysterious white house in woodland near Mapledurham in Oxfordshire. She was last seen 150 years ago with her beloved black cat. That was until I recognised her on the front cover of Black Sabbath's first album - as she was when she was young, but this photo was taken in 1970! Cue 'Twilight Zone' music. Now I knew why I was born to be a rocker.

Great grandmother Lowe...

My Great Grandmother in 1856	Great Grandmother on front of Black Sabbath's first album – released 1970

Maybe I should enquire as to if there are any royalty payments to be had? But then again those helpful bods from Sabbath – for some unknown reason – may not believe the validity of my claim. But hey, all is not lost – I still have the cat. Cue more 'Twilight Zone' music.

Why Such A Connection? Part 2

To me, rock music acted like a safe house – it allowed me to hide away from everything that I felt threatened by.

At the musical level I felt a sense that this was how music was meant to be; this was how instruments should be played. I was scathing of the pussy footing around that groups in the charts seemed to display with their instruments. The energy in my music, rock music, went straight into my ears, down my spinal cord, set my nerve ends alight and then docked perfectly with my frustrations.

At a much deeper level the culture of rock music really connected with who I was, or rather who I wanted to be - the clothes, the hair, the rebellion, the freedom and the sticking two fingers up to the establishment while at the same time not bothering to find out what the establishment really stood for. In effect rock music allowed me to bury my head in the sand. Below the surface of the sand I found something that made much more sense than anything I had encountered in the 'real' world.

And then, when I came up for air I was able to externally display who I was. And it seemed that the club to which I had become a member was far more exclusive and mysterious than other clubs. This gave me confidence because it didn't matter that the majority of my fellow pupils didn't get rock music; in fact the realisation that most of my fellow pupils didn't 'get' me – the real me, made the music even more appealing.

The next day at school after the Deep Purple incident I informed my (soon to be) old mates (Rob et al) that they were no longer cool and I was joining up with the rock-heads. The only trouble was, after a quick reconnaissance exercise, I discovered there weren't any other rock-heads at the Grange, so I went back to my (soon to be) old mates (Rob et al) and informed them that even though they weren't cool I would still be their friend. And so I waited for others to find rock. Soon enough this happened and I gradually moved away from Rob et al, and the Grange rock-clique formed. This comprised of Kev and me. And for a while it was great and I was in a much happier state of frustration and negativity. But something was still missing.

Chapter 15

Friend Will Be Friends

It was July 1975 and for some strange reason I found myself in a competition to see who could lob a flat spherical object the furthest. I was at the inter-school athletics meeting being held at King Edward VI sports field. The college is located in Stourbridge and a certain Robert Anthony Plant was a former pupil.

My eyes which had been focussed yonder as part of my mental preparation - or to put it another way, I was bored so I was assessing if there was any decent chicks floating around - now became fixed on a familiar face. Suddenly I was drawn like a magnet to the force of my visual connection.

"Hi Huw, how're you doing?"

"Paul," he replied in a refreshingly familiar tone.

"Pete," I replied in a tone that virtually ignored his name-to-face error.

"Yes, I meant Pete, how the devil are you Pete?" In synchronisation with his reply Huw scratched his head (he had clearly made some anatomical progress since infant school).

It had been two years since I failed my 11-plus and we'd gone our separate ways, but it was soon like old times! We quickly skirted over the boring discus talk and moved onto the much more interesting subject of…rock music. Huw had also been subject to the *'older brother syndrome'* and had already begun to embrace the rock scene. We reformed an immediate bond and arranged to meet up later that week to listen to each other's albums.

Very soon Huw introduced me to his 'newly converted' rock mates - Steve and Paul – who, by way of passing their 11-plus, were, like Huw, pupils at the King Edward VI grammar school.

One evening we listened to (the recently released) *Physical Graffiti* by Led Zeppelin. We sat there in total silence and I knew intuitively that these guys were going to be my soul mates – they were on my exact wavelength – demonstrating a perfect balance in terms of respect and passion for the music while at the same time not taking things (and especially ourselves) too seriously.

The next school day after the Led Zeppelin event I informed my (soon to be) old rock mate (Kev) that he was a rock loser and I was joining up with my new 'ever so cool' rock-head mates. I soon realised that decision left me with no mates at The Grange, because my old mates (Rob et al) were no longer speaking to me. So I went back to my old rock mate (Kev) and informed him that I would still be his friend, and that *I* was in fact the rock loser not him. He didn't buy it but we still remained good mates until we eventually lost touch after leaving school (see Chapter 2).

The rock genre encompasses a very broad congregation in terms of its sound and there are many sub-categories including Blues, Heavy Rock, Rock-blues, Progressive Rock, Pomp Rock, Jazz Rock,

AOR (Album or Adult Orientated Rock), American Rock, Southern American Rock, Pop Rock and Glam Rock to name but a few.

Apart from Glam Rock, which I wasn't really keen on, I embraced all forms of the rock brand and loved every note of the different sounds. My new mates, Huw, Paul and Steve, tended to have more specific tastes and had come to rock from a variety of different routes. Huw leaned more towards the progressive-rock side of the genre. Whereas Steve who lived opposite Huw wasn't so much into the heavy stuff like Black Sabbath or Deep Purple but more the bluesy side of rock, such as Hendrix and Clapton. Paul had been influenced by acts that had appeared on Top of the Pops and actually admitted to liking the Rubettes. The 'rockier' pop acts like Slade then replaced his Rubettes affliction and then his friendship with Huw moved him onto the next level...although Paul never lost his leanings towards the pop side of rock. So, between us we had an eclectic mix of rock tastes, but if you put on a benchmark album like the aforementioned *Physical Graffiti* then all tastes would unite in an unbridled appreciation of the sound.

The Rocker's Bedroom Antics Exposed

Back in 1975 rock music was a lot more mysterious than it is now. It was an understanding thing, or lack of it as the case may be. In a sense, we were like a secret sect, a Priory of Sion, in which most of our worshipping went on behind closed doors (our bedroom), where we kneeled (headbanged) and prayed (played our air guitar) to our rock gods (Jimi Hendrix, Jimmy Page et al) and worshipped our rock goddesses (or rock goddess to be exact as there was only Kate Bush, who's music we somehow managed to shoehorn into the rock brand – I wonder why?). Then, in the real world, we would be very insular, with no attempt to try and convert those who didn't believe. In fact it was the complete opposite - our perception being that the more people that didn't 'get it' the better.

However, in the mid-1970s two factors conspired to bring our secret deification out in the open. Firstly a few of our favourite bands decided to have a break from their self-imposed avoidance of the singles chart and they would sometimes even appear on Top of the Pops. Secondly the local disco scene came along. And that meant girls. So we crawled from under our duvets and made our way to the community disco venues. And gradually a small section of the pop-orientated evening started to get set aside for rock songs that were in or had been in the Top 40 singles chart. For example: *Layla*, *All Right Now*, *Down Down*, *Smoke on the Water*. And as it was compulsory to headbang whenever a rock song was heard, our bedroom behaviour was outed.

Headbanging Explained

Headbanging and its close relative, the air guitar, are essential skills to master if one is to become a legend amongst one's rock-following peers. To the dedicated rocker, headbanging is as natural a reaction as kicking out your lower leg when tapped on the knee, or whipping your knob out when Kate Bush appears on TV. You don't think about it, you can't resist it, you can't prevent it, it just happens, and it is part of your physiology. That's why rockers are rockers, because they can't help themselves. The music will find the person, not the other way round.

But the biomechanics of headbanging isn't as simple as it looks and, just like any other skill in life, there exists a multiplicity of skill levels. There are those who it comes naturally to – the Nureyev's of headbanging if you like. There are those who develop a good style after much practice and those who look like they are auditioning for a part in *One Flew over the Cuckoo's Nest*. Whatever the natural headbanging gifts a rocker is born with, when the music starts, the head will bang - period.

The general rule of thumb is the headbanging cadence needs to be andante (slow tempo) during the rhythm parts of the music, but then much more allegro (brisk tempo) during the guitar solos. However the exception to this rule is if the rhythm part is particularly frenetic in which case a free and easy form of improvisation can be adopted.

Headbanging together with the obligatory air-guitar are how the internal ecstasy that the music creates manifests itself on the outside. You're making a statement that you are connecting with what the band is playing. You know the chords or the solo and what's more you can play the damn thing with your eyes closed! I used to go mental when I was headbanging and I wanted to be (or at least thought I was) one of the most animated headbangers around. After all, I needed to be good at something.

In addition, one of the peripheral reasons why headbangers like rock is because fundamentally those who follow rock have no natural rhythm. Which isn't a hinderance with rock music because when it comes to the beat of a song headbanging involves virtually no coordination of upper and lower limbs whatsoever. It simply requires the adoption of the most outrageous and exaggerated guitar pose (i.e. legs wide apart). Then you're ready to go. Of course there are some tricky bits; you need to ensure that your back arches and your head tilts back during the high notes of a guitar solo and even drop to your knees if it's a particularly classic solo. But basically, legs apart and arms in the air-guitar position should do it. The more advanced exponents of the air-guitar learn to express the ecstasy of the guitar solo in a pained open mouthed expression that flows in perfect harmony with the notes of the solo. Or to put it another way, it looks like they're having a blow job. 🙊 Cue awkward, uncomfortable silence.

Summer 1975 – A Musical Benchmark In My Life

I soon learned that on TV the best source of innovation was The Old Grey Whistle Test (TOGWT). One broadcast was to have a significant impact on my life. It occurred in 1975 and featured a relatively unknown band (in the UK) called Lynyrd Skynyrd. I'd heard about this band whose reputation for bar-room brawls and general good old fashioned *fun* went before them. Word on the street was that they had a mind-blowing anthem. This Southern American band was appearing live on TOGWT. I had very rarely sat through a whole episode of the programme because all too often there was some boring crap on it like Kevin Ayers or Val Doonican. At the dismissive age of 13, my simple philosophy was, if it wasn't rock it wasn't worth listening to, even if I liked it! But tonight I was going to give it my best shot and stay up until the final credits.

It was approaching what I knew to be the last 15 minutes of the broadcast and if I'm honest I thought they were bloody good, but not up to Sabbath or Zeppelin standards. That was until this great slide guitar started and I had a feeling. It's hard to explain. I just knew something special was about to happen. This was the first time I heard *Freebird*.

The first two verses transfixed me. I was spellbound. There was the diminutive, but oh so cool lead singer, Ronnie Van Zant, with either side of him the two lead axemen, Allen Collins and Gary Rossington.

The second verse starts to shift in tempo and then Ronnie cries out: *"Lord help me, I can't chang,a,a,a,a,ange……Oh won't you fly....oh freebird, yea."*

As the guitar came in every hair on my body stood to attention. This wasn't one of those watershed moments in life - it was a fully-fledged reservoir-mansion. My excitement was of such magnitude that during the Allen Collins 10 minute epic guitar solo I was leaping around in random manic movements, not quite knowing what to do with my new found sense of euphoria. To this day that transition from vocals into the guitar section still makes the hairs on the back of my neck stand up - even though I've listened to the track a thousand times since that first hearing.

The next day I was beside myself with excitement and took the unprecedented step of phoning Huw before school.

"Can I speak to Huw please?" I mumbled.

"Who?"

"Yes Huw." It was a silly joke that never really worked, but I could never resist it "Sorry to bother you Mr M, it's Pete, is Huw there?"

"I'll get him," Mr M replied while simultaneously letting out an early morning disapproving sigh.

"Pete?" Huw came on the phone.

"Did you see it?"

"See what?" Huw had clearly inherited his Dad's ability to talk and sigh at the same time.

"The Old Grey Whistle Test last night, Lynyrd Skynyrd, Freebird, absolutely mind-blowing, breathtaking, awesome." My adjectives were sapping my energy. "Meet me after school in town; we have to find their album with this track on."

Before he had chance to reply I had put the phone down and I was on my way to school to daydream another day away.

After school I met up with Huw, Paul and Steve and we made a B-line for our local record store in Stourbridge.

"Leonard who?" said the soul-boy behind the counter.

"Lynyrd Skynyrd" I replied courteously.

"Lennord Skinhead?" he replied in manner that indicated the music shop had not sent him on a customer care course.

"No, it's pronounced Lynyrd Skynyrd." I remained calm.

"Never 'eard of 'em mate," he replied in a manner that indicated the music shop must have received only one application when the job of sales assistant came up.

"Can it be ordered?" I gave him the best Steve Martin pained expression I could muster, the one where his lips curl up, his eyes narrow and his brow furrows.

"I'll have a look, what's the name of the album?"

This was going to be fun.

"It's 'Pronounced Leh-*nerd* Skin-*nerd*'," I said.

"Look you cheesedick, you've told me the name of the band, now what's the name of the album."

Now in my experience of the retail trade, calling a potential customer a cheesedick was not conducive to securing a sale, but hey, he obviously had his own way of doing things.

"It's 'Pronounced Leh-nerd Skin-nerd'," I said again.

"Are you brain dead or has your fu…… or has your needle stuck?"

This time I spelled it out straight, "The album is called 'Pronounced Leh-nerd Skin-nerd'." I couldn't help but wonder to myself what species of Homosapien I was talking to.

"Okay, smart arse, what label is it on?" he had me on that one and I could see he was getting really agitated now so I decided my reply needed a degree of calming diplomacy.

"I don't know," was the best calming diplomacy I could think of, so to back it up I gave him the best Steve Martin puppy-dog expression I could muster - the one where his lips curl up, his eyes narrow and his brow furrows. Soul-boy looked at me in a way that meant that the only thing preventing me from getting a good hiding was him needing the job.

Needless to say I left empty-handed.

The following weekend I ventured into Birmingham and purchased the album, called 'Pronounced Leh-nerd Skin-nerd', from a better stocked record shop. I played the track to the lads with such pride that you'd have thought I'd written it myself.

The Wonder Of Vinyl

There was a time in the '70s when the coolest thing you could be seen with was not the latest fashion from the King's Road but the mysterious item that you carried under your arm. It was 130g of acetate and vinyl mix, it contained 1600 feet of groove and it was recognisable only to those who *understood*. It was of course the vinyl album and in my opinion the long-playing record is one of the most wonderful creations in the history of art.

The album was first unveiled by Columbia Records in 1948 and initially albums were a compilation of singles or a soundtrack from a musical, but this changed radically in the 1960s with rock orientated albums embracing concepts and containing tracks that would last a whole side. This intrinsically meant that albums weren't played on mainstream radio and so would be tagged as underground music operating outside mainstream culture. This ensured the long playing record would become the most revered possession of the dedicated follower of music. Such was the kudos of the album over the '45' vinyl single that Led Zeppelin famously refused to release singles – a template that was followed by many rock bands in the 1970s. The vinyl album allowed bands to express themselves and show off their musical abilities. The single was looked down on as a medium that undermined and limited creative expression.

As a consumer of vinyl delicacies I would embrace the search for an album as if it was the 'Holy Grail,' with a journey often embracing sorties to the back streets of Birmingham to spend hours in specialist record shops like Reddington's Rare Records (Moor Street) or The Diskery (Bromsgrove Street). On the return train journey all the sleeve notes would be devoured and the 'non believers' would look at the album cover with puzzlement - the designs of which were just magnificent visual treats. I loved the art work with the same passion as I loved the music.

My Top Five Album Covers of All Time

1. *Rainbow - Rainbow Rising. 1976. Album Cover: Ken Kelly*
2. *Meatloaf - Bat Out of Hell. 1977. Album Cover: Richard Corben*
3. *Derek and the Dominos - Layla and Other Assorted Love Songs. 1970. Album Cover: A painting by French Artist, Frandsen De Schonberg*
4. *Pink Floyd - The Dark Side of the Moon. 1973. Album Cover: Designed by Hipgnosis - Storm Thorgerson*
5. *King Crimson - In the Court of the Crimson King. 1969. Album Cover: Barry Godber*

Chapter 16

The Gig Scene
(1977)

Lynyrd Skynyrd - 2nd Feb 1977
(Birmingham Odeon, £1.40, Rear Stalls, MM8)

There was no last minute decision to be made with this gig. As soon as the tickets came on sale we got the best seats we could afford. Ever since the summer of 1975 when I first saw Skynyrd on The Old Grey Whistle Test I'd hoped that one day I would get a chance to see the band live.

This was Skynyrd's 'On The British Road' tour and when these guys were on the road, no groupie, no bottle of Jack Daniels and no TV set was safe. This band was the stuff rock legends were made of.

Other than a brief tour in which they appeared on the same bill as the Rolling Stones at Knebworth (1976) and supported and subsequently blew off stage Golden Earring, this was Skynyrd's first headlining tour of the UK.

Paul's dad was giving us a lift to the station but when I approached the car there was no "Hello, how you doing?" Just a Volvo full of laughing teenagers.

"I thought it had died!" More laughter followed Paul's subtle observation that I was wearing my Afghan for the first time since the Steve Hillage gig some six weeks before.

But this time I had something special up my sleeve (or on my back as was the case).

I quickly turned round with my back to the lads, placed my feet apart and opened the coat like a flasher who had not quite mastered the dynamics of his trade. There proudly displayed on the back of my Afghan was the Confederate flag that my lovely mother had sewn on. In truth I knew this might up the level of joviality, but in a way it deflected from the actual coat itself and the flag became the centre of attention. Of course, at that age I had absolutely no idea it was the Confederate flag, as far as I was concerned it was simply Skynyrd's logo!

When we arrived at the Odeon we made our way to our seats and were soon watching – for the second time (as a support act) - Clover. As with the previous time, (supporting Thin Lizzy), they were receiving a lukewarm reception and for the first time in our concert-going careers we decided to go to the bar and see if we could get a drink. Six months after promising myself *never* to show disrespect to the support bands, I was standing up and turning my back on a performance.

Up until now drink had played a bit-part in our lives. Yes, I'd had a mishap with cider at a party once, but that was the exception rather than the rule. Lately, as we were starting to look older, we were gaining in confidence and directing our attention to actually getting a drink in a pub. And one pub in Old Swinford, near Stourbridge, was known on the grapevine as a dead-cert to get an 'underage drink.' Ironically it was run by an ex-copper called Gordon. So, The Swan (now a restaurant called *Grill-it*) was the first pub we ever went into. Later on in our drinking careers, Gordon would occasionally let us in on a *lock-in*. It doesn't sound much now with 24-hour opening hours, but a *lock-in* in those days was living life on the edge.

So there we were, sat in a circle on the carpet in the Odeon bar having managed to secure one pint of beer between us. It was a good opportunity to plan tactics. Our four seats were downstairs towards the back of the cinema.

"We've gotta be ready for any sudden movements," I said as if this was a serious military exercise. "I don't think the crowd are gonna hang around tonight, I can just feel it."

"Shall we just run to the front before the lights go down?" Huw said from the comfort zone of the bar. Relatively experienced concert goers we may have been, but we were still young compared to most of the crowd, so to make such a bold move seemed beyond our station at that stage.

"Okay, we'll follow you," I said to Huw with a slight garnish of sarcasm.

"Okay, what then?" Huw retorted with a seasoning of aggression to counter the sarcasm.

An eerie silence befell our circle.

"I have a plan." Paul got the conversation back on track. Paul always had a plan. "Let's all fix on a position to watch for any runners, I'll look to the front, Huw you look to the right, Steve you look to the left and Pete, you look to the back. Any sign of a run to the front, shout out and we'll follow."

It sounded a reasonable plan in principle, until I realised something.

"What happens if no one makes a move until halfway through the gig, by then I'll not only have missed half the gig but the guy behind me will probably think I fancy him!"

We laughed and eventually after about 20 minutes of intense brainstorming we came up with no plan whatsoever. We went back into the arena, took our seats, shouted out a few "Heinz Baked Beans" and waited for Lynyrd Skynyrd. Sitting there, I felt an excited knot of anticipation in my stomach; I was so much up for this gig.

When the lights went down it was as if all the audience had agreed to run to the front simultaneously but had failed to include us in their plans. All it took was the slightest dimming of the lights to trigger an almighty charge. In all the gigs I'd been to so far I'd never known anything like it. After all our discussions on tactics we were caught off guard and we had to sprint with all our youthful speed in order to gain a decent position at the front. As soon as the opening notes sounded to "Call me the Breeze" we were a sea of no nonsense, headbanging, arms waving, rock heads – conscripts to the Yankee cause. Eighty minutes later and the band finally yielded to the cries that had been emanating from the crowd all night.

"What song is it you wanna hear?" cried out Ronnie Van Zant.

They did a 14-minute version of *Freebird* and just in case someone in the crowd had thought they were a bit light on guitarists (they had three in the band) a guest guitarist called Pete came on from the aptly named Climax Blues Band. By this stage we had pushed and cajoled our way between rows C and D and such was my feeling of apotheosis at hearing Freebird that it must have looked like I was having a fit. But there was no loss of consciousness, in fact it was the complete opposite - there was an incredible sense of feeling alive. Music can do that to a person.

"That was the best ever, nothing will ever top that," I said almost before the lights went up. I'd said it after Be-Bop Deluxe, I'd said it after Rainbow and now I meant it with even more passion. We had seen something very, very special and it was great that we knew exactly how each other felt.

"Could have done with one more guitarist!" said Paul. We laughed like he had just told us the funniest joke in the world - a laughter based on adrenaline rather than humour.

Review from the Birmingham Evening Mail

Skyn head mania

Lynyrd Skynyrd, The Odeon, Birmingham.

AMERICAN rock band, Lynyrd Skynyrd, received a 90-minute standing ovation in Birmingham last night.

From the moment they appeared on stage at The Odeon hordes of fans leapt up to dance at the front, a sea of waving arms lashed into a frenzy by every note. And Skynyrd deserved it. They are the American equivalent of The Rolling Stones for stage excitement, their Deep South sound coming from somewhere below the gut.

There's no fancy Jagger tricks, just three (later four) lead guitarist and a keyboard player conjuring up a hypnotic assault on the senses backed by a solid drummer and bass.

Only at the end when they went over the top in their traditional encore tribute to Duane Allman, did the wall of sound block out the music.

Less exciting for the Skyn heads, was the supporting Californian group, Clover.

But they had more than three leaves to their rock score and superbly lead by pedal guitarist John McFree, produced a tight mixed bag varying from blues to country pickin' – and even yodelling.

BRIAN GLOVER

Little did we know how special (in a tragic way) that tour and that gig would turn out to be. Eight months later on October 20th 1977 the band's rented plane ran out of fuel and crashed into a swamp in Gillsburg, Mississippi. A number of the group and crew died including Ronnie Van Zant, lead singer and the main inspiration behind the band. It was a very sad day.

Chapter 17

Learning to Play the Guitar: Part 7

(First Live Gig, October 2001)

Somewhere in all the excitement of learning to play the guitar I got married, and as it was approaching our 40th birthdays I decided to arrange a surprise party for us both. Well, not much of a surprise for me, but one of us had to be in on the act. Birthday parties, of course, involve friends and family and for the evening I had hired a band that included a guitarist we knew. That's when I had the bright idea: I could perform a surprise gig. I'd now been playing the guitar for almost three years (yes, if nothing else, I'm a glutton for punishment) and most of my friends didn't even know I'd taken it up. I sat down and started to assess the logistics. Firstly I looked at the plus points:

- Plus point 1, I had a guitar.
- Plus point 2..........

Onto the negative points:

- I'm not a very good guitarist.
- I don't know any classic rock songs off-by-heart.
- I can't sing.

I assessed what I had written down. It didn't look good. There was only one thing for it, learn *Freebird*.

The thought of playing something simple never entered my head and if it did, it never registered. They say it is a trait of the Scorpion, but I don't believe in all that mumbo-jumbo. I put it down to a complete lack of common sense. Once again I was adhering to my tried and tested maxim: 'it's better to play a difficult song badly, than play an easy song badly.'

So my set at our surprise birthday party was to involve two songs. In addition to *Freebird*, the other song I'd selected was Santana's version of the classic Zombies song *She's Not There*. Equally suicidal, in musical terms, but it fitted nicely into my selection criteria. I purchased the backing tracks and the TAB and set about learning the two songs for my first ever live gig. I was about to go on tour!

The Night of the Gig (October 2001)

Friends and family arrived at the Jackson Tor Hotel in Matlock where we had booked the function room for the evening. The surprise part had gone really well and the band was coming to the end of their first set. All the usual suspects were there, including Huw, Steve and Paul. I'd arranged with the band that I would do my turn during their interval. It would have been great to have played the songs with the band, but there had been no time to meet up, let alone rehearse, so my first gig was to be with a backing track. I had also roped in my brother's trusty vocal talents.

I'd already lobbed the TV out of our hotel bedroom window so I was really starting to feel like a rock star.

I got up on stage and said my thanks to everyone for turning up and by now the audience were fully aware that I was a closet axe maniac and that their ears were about to receive a full on assault.

Then the backing track to *She's Not There* kicked in and my first gig had commenced. There was an immediate surge to the back with my new allegiance of fans falling over one another to escape. I hit my first solo with about 50% accuracy and by the second solo I'd stopped caring. There was enthusiastic applause at the end of the first number and I lapped it up as if it was heartfelt rather than its truer nature, sympathetic.

As *Freebird* kicked in the forgiving crowd hollered and applauded and I was really starting to enjoy it. By the time the solo came along I was postulating with my phallic penis (the guitar) at the front-of-stage groupie (the wife) and at that moment in time I wished I'd purchased a cucumber from the greengrocers. I was self-actualising on all cylinders and I was just in the middle of repeating the same short riff for the 100th time when Malc pulled out my guitar lead and held it up to the crowd as if it was the sword that had just slain the beast. Worryingly this received the biggest cheer of the night.

Shortly afterwards I was standing in the hotel toilet, looking at myself in the mirror. It was time for reflection.

Chapter 18

The Gig Scene
(1977 Continued – Age 15)

Black Sabbath - 6th March 1977
(New Bingley Hall, £2.00, Ticket No.4112)

I had been looking forward to the Sabbath gig for a long time. I missed Zeppelin and Purple, so Sabbath represented my only chance to see one of the 'big 3' before they split up or before one of the original members left. Of course, Sabbath and Purple would offer up many chances later on, as they reformed and performed with different line-ups, but to see one of the big 3 in their original phase was a must for any rock fan worth his salt.

But I have to say that it wasn't an all-time classic gig. Something wasn't quite right and later when I read about it I can see why. Tension and conflict between band members was rife, as was doing a lot of dope. In fact the following year Ozzy left Sabbath for three months and then he was fired on April 27, 1979. So all was not a happy camp leading up to this gig. To add to the woe Bingley Hall lacked the atmosphere of the Birmingham Odeon and so after the gig there wasn't the usual buzz in the car on the way home.

Stafford Bingley Hall was a 10,000 capacity shed (literally a great big cowshed), at the County Showground just outside Stafford. Maybe we were expecting too much or maybe it was a sign of a band that had run out of steam. The best gigs we had been to so far had involved bands that were just starting out on world domination like Rainbow and Skynyrd. It pains me to say it, but I felt the inspiration and the power that was synonymous with the Sabbath name just wasn't there. I mean, no virgins were sacrificed and all the Bingley Hall bats slept peacefully.

Pink Floyd - 28th March 1977
(New Bingley Hall, £3.50, Ticket No.20859)

Pink Floyd were touring to promote the 'Animals' album which was released on 23rd January 1977. They were riding high on the success of their previous two albums: *The Dark Side of the Moon* (1973) and *Wish You Were Here* (1975) and so this gig equated to our most expensive concert ticket to date.

A prog rock gig is much more a listening and visual experience than a hard rock gig, which means you get to watch the concert the whole way through rather than just the usual 50% that would be the norm when headbanging. Yes, at prog rock gigs we would never even think about running to the front and if you so much as dared to shout out Wally, you were immediately showered with pathos, and subject to mutterings of rock-dummy.

138

The Gig

This gig was the perfect opportunity to show we weren't just a bunch of mindless headbanging morons.

"That's a bloody pig and a half." I shouted to the lads, as a huge pink inflatable pig floated above us.

In preparation for shooting the cover of the *Animals* album plans were made to fly a forty-foot, helium-filled pink pig shaped balloon over Battersea Power Station. However the pig broke free due to a strong gust of wind and disappeared from sight, later being spotted by airline pilots at thirty thousand feet, with the result that flights at Heathrow Airport had to be cancelled. The flying pig finally landed on a rural farm in Kent and fathered many piglets (pigs will fly!)

"Yeah, very...pink," Huw replied with inspired observational skills.

"Almost Orwellian wouldn't you say?" A totally inappropriate use of my awareness of the inspiration behind *Animals*, but I'd been waiting to drop it in all night.

"Shall we go to the side and stand up? My arse is bloody killing me," Steve was clearly less enthusiastic about the pig and George Orwell.

For this gig the audience chose to sit and watch the spectacle rather than stand, which meant due to the lack of seating at the Bingley Hall the evening became a bit of an endurance test on the gluteus maximus.

"I'm with Steve," I shouted "my arse has gone uncomfortably numb!"

At that point we were near the mixing desk in the middle of the hall and I'm sure I heard Roger Waters' roadie say something like 'that's a good line, I must write it down' – but I could have been mistaken.

We enjoyed the gig immensely (as well as playing all of *Animals,* Floyd also played the whole of the *Wish You Were Here* album and finished with a track from *The Dark Side of the Moon* as an encore), but the big bands of that era, who had been around since the late 60s and early 70s, were starting to become old fashioned and they were coming under fire from the emerging punk-rock movement who saw them as flabby, pretentious and past their sell by date. This had dilemma written all over it. We didn't want to desert the prog rock brand, but at the same time we didn't want to come across as dated and undermine our potential to attract the opposite sex – as basically the only girls who were into prog rock were the intellectual types and so unless you were able to quote the entire works of Proust or be an expert in 3-man tag trigonometry then you were scuppered. We were scuppered. So after minutes of deliberation we decided to keep our prog rock predilections to ourselves and stick to the edgier, harder rock bands. However, although prog rock was the focus of the majority of punk's musical rebellious tones, they were none too polite about any brand of music that had been around for longer than a week and downright rude about bands that recorded tracks that lasted longer than a minute and that included the stalwarts of the heavy rock genre. Sometimes in life, you just can't win.

The Rock Music Fan

Rock music makes for an interesting fan base. Most musical genres have a following that is very much aligned with a particular class or culture. Think of northern soul, rap, punk, and classical music, but rock music cuts across the cultural and class differences of society and appeals to a much broader demographic – albeit a small percentage of each specific demographic sector. I.e. from the archetypal rock nerd who displays little in the way of social skills but finds his raison d'être through rock music, through to the equally nerdy but far more (academically) intellectual and usually middle class university types who take great delight in telling you how amazing the forty over three time signature is on a particular King Crimson track. That's one of the things I like about rock music: it appeals to a broad spectrum of people and therefore when defined as a single genre (rather than broken down into its various component parts), isn't so much defined by social class but by the music per se. I really should get out more.

Ian Gillan - 23rd May 1977

(Birmingham Odeon, £1.00, Rear Circle, V17)

It was the weekend after the Floyd gig and we had decided to stump up the princely sum of £1.00 to see the legendary Ian Gillan. One the punks would call a dinosaur for sure, but hey, I'd heard he played *Child in Time* so I felt compelled to go. And besides I wasn't a punk I was a rocker, so I wasn't going to be dictated to by a group of anti-establishment spikey heads. After all, rock was meant to be anti-establishment, but in a more establishment kind of way. Anyway, it was only a quid - what could go wrong.

The Gig

We arrived at the Birmingham Odeon and made our way upstairs to our seats and waited for the support band to come on; this was our first time in the circle.

"Just tell us in simple language...what the heck are we doing up here?" Steve said. This statement was the culmination of the last five minutes of mocking abuse I had endured for purchasing rear circle 'V' row seats.

"Look, a couple of weeks ago you were wondering if Gillan was past it and now you're telling me you're pissed off because I didn't get you seats near the front. I can't win." I was vying for the sympathy vote but it didn't work.

"Yes, but when we said we were up for it, we didn't mean it literally," said Paul. We all laughed at that one and it gave me a bit of breathing space to think.

"Look, I have a plan. Have you brought your Lynyrd Skynyrd tickets like I requested?" They all nodded. "Good, now have you noticed that just before the lights go down, the venue goes from half empty to full? Considering the gigs very rarely start on time, I've been wondering how people know when to arrive." I paused to make sure I knew where I was going. I hated long speeches.

"Well, when we went to see Lizzy, it suddenly became clear... Remember we sat in the bar and a bell rang? I wasn't sure what it meant at first as no one seemed to take any notice but then, I think it was the third ring, yes the third ring, the whole bar emptied and we quickly followed the crowd. Do you remember?"

They all nodded. "Well when we headed back inside, there was an almighty rush at the doors and the security men checking tickets didn't even bother looking at them, it would have taken too long. Most people just waved their tickets in the air and in they went; all the security guards were doing was making sure it was the right colour."

Three pairs of eyes looked at me as if I was about to tell them how to do it with a woman. Clearly, I needed to join all the dots.

"At Skynyrd, the whole crowd stood up when the lights went down and there was an almighty run to the front...yes?"

There was still no sound from my captive audience.

"Right, well this is my plan. After the support has finished, we'll go into the bar for a drink, then we'll wait for the bell to ring three times and join the rush to get in downstairs. We'll use our Skynyrd tickets so the security men can see we have the right colour ticket." I could detect from their expressions that the penny was beginning to drop. "Make sure you position yourself on the other side to where the security guy is standing and just wave it in the air as you go in."

The penny may have dropped, but it was still spinning round and had not yet come to rest. Huw was the first to speak.

"What happens if the lights don't go down straight away?"

"I'm guessing it's not a sell out, so we just take up the empty seats," I had spent many a waking hour in bed thinking this one through.

"Hahh…" Steve thought he had detected a flaw in my plan, "What happens if it is a sell out and either the lights don't go down straight away or if they do, no one runs to the front?"

As I said, I had spent many hours thinking this one through and imagining all scenarios.

"Well," I said with confidence, as it was important to have total self-belief in the plan to get them on board, "if that does happen then we can go to the bog and wait to hear the cheer of the crowd that signals the lights have gone down and… if there is no run to the front and no spare seats…well…we simply return back to our seats upstairs. They don't bother checking tickets on the way out."

They all nodded unconvincingly but because there were no holes left in my plan I could tell that they were going to place their trust in my judgement.

What followed would lift our egos to the outer planetary strata.

We sat on the carpet in the bar, forming a circle around the communal pint. It felt like we were naughty school boys up to no good and as we were still at school and we were up to no good (well, sort of) it was an appropriate feeling. There was an excitement in our circle and when the first bell sounded my heart missed a beat. The second bell seemed to take an eternity and by the time the third bell rang I felt like a nervous wreck. Thankfully, as predicted, all the people downed their drinks and headed for their seats. We latched on to the crowd heading for the stalls and as we approached the security guards my heart was racing.

145

People were entering the stalls through four separate doors and we split up and joined the queue to each door. The ticket inspectors were standing to the left of each door and as I joined the right hand side of the melee, I glanced to see that the lads had followed my instructions and were adopting similar positions. Everything then happened in a blur. I just kept my eyes to the front, kept a tight rein on those around me and held my ticket up in the air, waving it around as manically as possible. A part of me was waiting for the guard to shout "Oi, you," but there was no hand on the shoulder, no chastising voice, just the sight of a sea of rockers. It was important not to dwell, as this may have given the game away. As the lights were still on I made for the toilet.

One by one the lads joined me in the bog. I stood there at the left urinal with Steve the far side and Huw and Paul in the cubicles. I stood for what seemed like 10 minutes hoping George Michael didn't show up and then we heard the roar of the crowd. The lights must have gone down. Huw and Paul piled out of the traps and Steve joined us as we exited the toilets. The plan had been to walk out calmly and if everyone was still seated and there were no spare seats, then head back upstairs. But as I threw open the toilet door and we were greeted by the sheer power of the atmosphere, there was such a rush of adrenaline through my body that all the hours of mental rehearsal went flying out the window. The roar of the crowd had seemed so loud from inside the toilet that I'd convinced myself that the run-to-the-front must have already started and we were missing out on a prime position. So as we came out, running from the toilet, without pausing to assess the situation, we headed down the aisle. As my eyes adjusted from the light of the toilet to the darkness of the venue it quickly dawned on me that in fact no one had run to the front and everyone was still seated. Bloody hell, I was halfway down the top tier of the stalls, my three mates were behind me and we were committed to our run. For a split second of paranoia I was sure that all eyes were on me. My head was in turmoil, there were no spare seats and Gillan hadn't even come on yet. The whole situation was just about to exceed my problem-solving capabilities when the drummer banged out the beat to the first song. We were about 20 feet from the front stalls and on hearing this it just seemed to send a new rush of adrenaline through my body and my jog turned into a run. I could feel the lads behind me following suit. A wall of sound hit the arena as the rest of the band came on stage and the whole place lit up. Suddenly everyone saw the four of us running to the front and before I knew it rockers were leaping out of their seats from all directions and as we approached the front stalls the security guards didn't stand a chance.

We got a great position just in front of the stage and we were buzzing throughout the evening. It may not have been the greatest gig we ever went to, but for sheer *joie de vivre* it was one of the best. We hadn't even turned 16 and we had led the die hard rock fans to the stage. The flame of rock was still burning brightly and we were loving it......loving every minute of it.

Review from the Birmingham Evening Mail

Power still full on

Ian Gillan Band, Odeon, Birmingham
AFTER two years of silence, the voice that once belted out the lyrics for Deep Purple has lost none of its power.

Gillan proved what his supporters have always known – he ranks among the greats of rock screamers.

But last night's show was not all about one man, and the band played a set that had something for everyone.

For long periods Ray Fenwick dominated the stage, filling the air with some inspired extended riffs, and John Gustafson contributed a vocal performance that would keep a lesser man than Gillan looking over his shoulders.

A creditable first tour show from what will become a major band, despite the fact that on this occasion most of the applause was drawn for "oldies" like Child In Time.

Support group Strapps gave a good account of themselves, too.

BOB MULLETT

Chapter 19

Growing Up
(July 1977: Age 15. First Love)

There are a certain number of things a teenage male rock head needs: long hair, denim, a dislike of televisions and a rock-chick.

The most important criteria for the rock-chick is long hair, thigh length boots and a half-decent headbanging routine. In addition she needs to be individualistic and free-spirited. At least that's what I thought in those blinkered teenage rock years.

Now, here's the thing…this may have been nothing more than a perception or misperception as the case may have been but the only girls that seemed to be into rock music were either the intelligent types or the older types. In either case it meant I stood no chance. There was Jane Milton, our age, long-hair, down to earth, incredibly good looking. A rock-chick of breath-taking proportions. But there was about as much chance of me scoring with her as there was of the Pope appearing in *Debbie Does Dallas*.

Anyway, one day, totally out of the blue Steve, who was a year older than Huw, Paul and myself, got himself a girlfriend. A girl called Michelle. This brought our own 'girl-less' world into greater focus. We had hidden our prog rock albums and for Steve this had worked, but for us three really cool losers this gesture alone wasn't enough to stimulate a rush of chicks. We were going to need to make additional sacrifices. And clearly at some point I was going to have to talk to a girl.

It was a Thursday evening during the school holidays and Steve, Huw and Paul were in my bedroom listening to the new album by Rush.

"Steve?"

"Yeeeaaasssss?" That extended 'yes' indicated that he was already suspicious of what I might ask.

"Does Michelle have any rock-chick mates?" This was a serious subject - there was no point in beating about the bush.

"Funny, you should ask that…" We all straightened our backs in anticipation.

"I asked her that exact same question last night." We pricked our ears in further anticipation.

"And?" Our noses were now twitching. Steve had this smug look on his face that indicated he knew he was in possession of some priceless information. He let it punctuate the moment.

"She knows Jane Milton." Talk about throwing the dog(s) a bone; we were running round in circles, shouting and screaming, like he'd just told us Robert Plant was at the front door.

Like I alluded to earlier Jane Milton was the archetypal rock-chick, every young rock-head in Stourbridge worth his salt knew of her. In fact coming to think of it, she wasn't far off Robert Plant in terms of her local legendary status. We were all firing questions at Steve at varying levels of intensity, volume and animation. He raised his arms and gestured with his palms facing downwards for us to calm down. "Michelle is going with Jane and another friend to the Stourbridge swimming baths tomorrow."

It was as if he'd thrown a pile of fire-crackers into the middle of us. After about 10 minutes we'd calmed down enough to find out what time they were going and to arrange our own *rendezvous* for tomorrow's trip to the swimming baths. We also told Steve not to tell Michelle we were coming.

The Next Day at the Swimming Pool

Despite our childish bedroom excitement, in the outside world we had to keep our cool rock-heads firmly screwed on. We didn't want it to look like we had gone to the pool especially to gawk at Jane, so we got there 10 minutes early to gawk at the other girls instead. And then they appeared from the girls' changing room. There was Michelle, Jane and one of their friends who none of us had seen before. As they walked past us Michelle said hello to Steve, while we gawked open-mouthed at Jane. It was 'periscope up' time for Paul and Huw, who on seeing Jane in her swimming costume needed to dive, dive, dive and did indeed dive straight into the pool. I would have joined them, but my attention had been distracted by their mystery friend.

It was difficult to assess rock-chick potential in the swimming pool, as unfortunately thigh length boots weren't the normal swimming costume accessory. However I did notice the mystery girl had really nice red hair, but because she had obviously showered before entering the pool it was difficult to gauge its exact length or style and therefore rock-chick potential.

As they walked down the poolside, the mystery friend definitely looked back at me from over her shoulder and my heart skipped a beat. Was she looking at me? I was sure she was looking at me. But then again? But yes, but no. Yes. But no. Yes. No. Bollocks…she was *definitely* looking at me.

I majestically belly flopped into the pool to join my mates. They were all talking about Jane. I interrupted their flow.

"Did you see that?"

"See what?" replied Steve.

"Jane's friend, she gave me the eye." I said it with a strange seriousness that for a moment changed the atmosphere. It was as if, deep down inside, I'd already let this person into my heart.

"What's her name?" Huw initially directed the question at me, but realising that I obviously wouldn't know, he quickly changed his glance towards Steve.

"I don't know. Do you want me to go and find out?" replied Steve.

I looked at him straight in the eye. There was a pause as I gave myself a quick pep talk: *Don't be a loser, don't ask Steve to do it…just swim confidently over to her and ask her out. What could be simpler? You can't rely on other people for the rest of your life. Be a man.*

"Go on then. Thanks Steve, oh, and while you're there will you ask her if she wants to go out with me?"

Steve swam off shaking his head at my lack of bottle and then a few minutes later returned from his reconnaissance mission, "Her name's Viv and she said yes."

"What do you mean yes? What did she say?" I couldn't believe it; he must have got it wrong.

"I just told you, she said yes."

"Yes to what?" Blind stupidity seems an inevitable reaction when you have just been struck with Cupid's arrow. I knew the answer, but I had to make sure that when he asked her, he didn't throw in a word that could be misconstrued.

"Yes, to your question – will she go out with you?" I could tell the boys' empathy was starting to wear thin and I was starting to lose face. It was time for me to act.

"What shall I do now?" My *face* was well and truly lost.

"Go and talk to her you dormitory." This was a curious turn of phrase from Huw and one that I'd never heard him say before or since, but I was too excited to question its metaphorical or social-psychological context.

Up until now I had kept my excruciating shyness when confronted with a girl pretty much under wraps. Now Huw, Steve and Paul were witnessing first-hand what a complete wimp I was when it came to the opposite sex. Before I'd had time to compose myself I saw through the corner of my eye Viv swimming over towards me and I entered an unparalleled state of panic, as if a demented Miss Havisham was coming towards me hungry for her 'shy-boy' breakfast. I panicked. I couldn't have my big moment witnessed by everyone, so I swam off as if I hadn't seen her coming. I was beside myself with inner turmoil. I felt like I was going to lose the girl of my dreams before I'd even said hello to her. I was desperately waiting for the moment when there would be clear water between her and anyone else. Then it happened, Jane and Michelle got out of the water and left Viv on her own in what looked like a well-rehearsed plan to see if I was willing to enter the last chance saloon. So I swung open the doors and swam over – but I had no idea what I was going to say.

"Hi, I hear you want to go out with me."

I looked at her and smiled pathetically. There was a pause and it gave me a chance to give myself another pep talk: *You stupid idiot, you asked her out, well Steve did, she didn't ask you out. Look at her, she's gobsmaked. You really are a dipshit.*

She chose to ignore my oversight and broke the silence.

"Yes."

Three letters that defy the emotions such a small word can create. Just to hear a feminine voice say 'yes', was enough to send me into melt-down.

"Great, I'm Pete." I was quickly descending into rock-loser territory and this wasn't helped by the fact I held out my hand to shake hers.

"Yes I know, your friend told me. I'm Viv." She gently shook the tips of my rock-loser fingers. Even that was enough to stir a reaction below deck. I adjusted my swimming trunks.

"What about meeting tonight?" Keeping them keen wasn't one of my strong points.

"Can't tonight, going out." Her eyes told me she was telling the truth.

"What about tomorrow?"

"Can't tomorrow, going to watch a play at Stourbridge Town Hall." There was enough additional information to convince me that this also was the truth.

"What about Sunday?"

"Sorry can't make that day either."

I was beginning to realise how John Cleese's character felt from the *Cheese Shop* sketch. But she had said 'yes', so I was keen to keep guessing which day would be the special day and whether it would be this year or next. I had images of the pool lights going out with just the two of us in the water and me up to Christmas and Viv still saying no, but in a highly genuine and convincing way. But these thoughts were quickly interrupted.

"Wait a minute, Sunday, yes, I can make Sunday." I made another adjustment to my swimming trunks.

I didn't want to get involved in a proper conversation, so as soon as we had arranged the Sunday meeting venue - the bandstand in Mary Stevens Park, Stourbridge - I quickly retreated back to the lads. I had never felt such excitement in all my life and I still hadn't seen her with her clothes on! I was presuming she was into rock as she was with Jane and Michelle, who we knew were rock-chicks, but I wasn't 100% certain. The doubt in my mind created a great deal of anxiety, as the last thing I wanted was to meet a girl and not be able to talk solely about rock music.

****

Footnote: Needless to say none of us ever 'scored' with Jane Milton. And after we left school, she disappeared off the radar altogether...paradise lost.

The Evening after the Swimming Pool

That evening the lads and I were off to a rock-disco in Stourbridge. The local disco scene was still primarily a tottie-touting exercise, but at least the music side of the scene had diversified into specialised areas of musical taste, hence the crucial *rock* before the *disco*. Tonight I was there solely for the music, because as far as I was concerned I had a steady girlfriend.

We had been there about 10 minutes and I was just in the middle of my headbanging warm-up routine, when Huw came running over.

"Pete, Pete, guess what?" I didn't have time to answer. "She's here; she's here at the disco."

"Who?" The penny had genuinely not dropped.

"Vivien, the girl you asked out today, she's here at the disco."

I was primed for many things Huw might have said, but this wasn't one of them. I was overcome with excitement and fear. I grabbed Huw by the shoulders.

"She's here – are you sure?"

"Definitely, she looks totally different; she's got masses of red hair." I was desperately trying to assimilate all this information into something that would make sense and more importantly give clarity to my next move.

"Where is she?" I asked.

Huw pointed to the other side of the room, beyond the crowd of people in the middle. She was out of view. It was time for me to show the real me. This was my patch, my comfort zone. I was surrounded by mates, rockers and loud heavy-rock music. If I couldn't be myself in this environment I would be forever hiding behind my self-doubt. I looked at Huw's urging eyes and I knew what he was thinking. He was right, this was my moment...now was the time. *Layla* suddenly blasted out from the speakers and it seemed to inject 10 grams of courage into my veins. My first ever date awaited.

To say I was taken aback is an understatement; she was wearing tight jeans and a lose fitting green top and she had gorgeous long, curly, red hair. If she had been wearing the proverbial thigh length boots I would have asked her to marry me there and then.

I instantly felt comfortable with Vivien and we talked all night about rock music – once I remember she tried to change the subject, but I quickly returned it back to rock. I was in heaven. That night, aged 15 and a half, I had my first ever kiss. The tongue was a bit of a surprise as I'd always assumed you just sat there, touched lips and moved your head from side to side, but hey, I was kissing a rock-chick, in a rock disco, I wasn't going to ask for an instruction manual.

And after that we danced – my first ever dance with a girl. I was rubbish but I didn't care. All I knew was that in that moment I felt like a king. We ended up meeting every night that weekend and there is something very special about that moment, when for the first time in your life, another person enters your heart in a way that you could never have imagined.

I'm going to include some lyrics by a well-known country singer that - at this juncture of the story - fit perfectly. Of course, country music isn't rock music but good lyrics are good lyrics and sometimes you have to diversify in order to make a point (bollocks of course, but I had to come up with some excuse for including them).

Looking back on the memory of
The dance we shared 'neath the stars above
For a moment all the world was right
How could I have known that you'd ever say goodbye

And now I'm glad I didn't know
The way it all would end the way it all would go
Our lives are better left to chance
I could have missed the pain
But I'd have had to miss the dance

Holding you I held everything
For a moment wasn't I a king
But if I'd only known how the king would fall
Hey who's to say you know I might have changed it all

Yes my life is better left to chance

© *Garth Brooks   "The Dance" (Lyrics shortened)*

Chapter 20

The Gig Scene
(1977 Continued)

TOWN HALL, BIRMINGHAM

HARVEY GOLDSMITH ENTERTAINMENTS
By Arrangements with CBS Records presents

**C R A W L E R   B O X E R
M O O N**

FRIDAY, 22nd JULY, 1977,
at 1930 hours

GROUND FLOOR   **£1.00**

PLEASE RETAIN
LATECOMERS will not be admitted until a convenient
break in the programme. Tickets cannot be exchanged or
money refunded.

Crawler, Boxer, Moon - 22nd July 1977
(Birmingham Town Hall, £1.00, Ground Floor, C6)

Friday 22nd July 1977 represented a significant moment in my concert-going career. I had my jeans, I had my badges, I had my patches, I had my concert t-shirts, I had my longish hair, I had my seriously honed headbanging routine, I had my eclectic mix of 'Wally' shouts. It was time I had, by my side, my … rock-chick!

Vivien and I had been going out for exactly one week and to celebrate our one week anniversary I was taking her to a rock gig.

Admittedly, the line-up may have been a bit obscure to all but the most die-hard rock fans. But beneath the obscurity there was some quality. The headliners were Crawler, who had morphed out of Back Street Crawler, the late great Paul Kossoff's band. Paul Kossoff had originally been the lead guitarist in Free. After his sad demise due to drug-related heart problems, the remainder of the band continued as Crawler. Boxer too, had some very respectable musicians. And Moon were a seven piece funk-rock band who opened the show.

By the end of the gig I was ecstatic, the best £2.00 I'd ever spent! I even got a seat near the front to impress my new found concert going companion, or to put it another way, I didn't want to have to expose her to the 'running from the cheap seats to the front' culture too soon.

By the end of the night Vivien knew exactly what she had let herself in for, as I felt it my duty, as the experienced concert-goer, to point out and over-act all the concert going clichés. How embarrassing it is to think that I called out '*Wally*' first, stood up first and then headbanged my way through the whole gig, occasionally coming up for air to ask Vivien if she was enjoying herself. I sure knew how to impress a girl. That said, purely from a live gig perspective it was great and I still have the free EP which they gave out on the night - in which the Boxer track, called *No Reply* from their album 'Absolutely', is a classic, with two great guitar solos. In truth though, to those whose critical faculties were located between their ears, not in their heart, they may have found the quality of the majority of the songs average, but that evening, to my ears, every track was a classic.

We caught the No.9 bus from the centre of Birmingham back to Quinton to meet up with my mother. On the bus we were on a real high.

"That's the best gig I've ever been to." What was I saying! Having been to see the likes of Rainbow, Lizzy, Skynyrd and Sabbath, there was something definitely wrong with me. I felt very strange.

"It was ace, I loved the freaking out bit." She replied.

I hadn't heard the term 'ace' used to describe a gig before, but it seemed just the perfect word to use. My God, something was definitely wrong with me.

"Vivien," my heart was beating so loud I was sure she could hear it.

"Yes Pete." I was putty, pure putty, absolutely helpless and right there on the romantic setting of the Quinton 9 bus I had to say it.

"I love you."

Each word seemed to release about 10 gallons of blood through my veins. It was one of those moments when you enter a parallel world, in which everything around you seems to be happening at a different speed. I had always imagined what it would be like to say those words, what it would feel like and now I knew and it was the best feeling in the world. Better than hearing Deep Purple for the first time and even better than hearing *Freebird*. But nothing, no nothing could have prepared me for the emotions I felt when Vivien replied "I love you too."

ODEON THEATRE
BIRMINGHAM

ENDALE presents
TED NUGENT

Rear Circle
£2.00

U 29

Thur. Aug. 18
at 7.30 p.m.

No ticket exchanged nor money refunded
This portion to be retained   [P.T.O.]

Ted Nugent - 18th Aug 1977

(Birmingham Odeon, £2.00, Rear Circle, U29)

It was early August 1977 - Vivien and I were walking through Mary Stevens park in Stourbridge.

"Honestly, he's not that loud at all, he's more a ballad man. I mean, he's called Ted...like Ted Heath. Just an old timer really." Having had such a good time at the Boxer, Crawler, Moon gig and having declared our undying love for one another, I now offered Vivien first refusal on the gig scene. In truth, for the Ted Nugent concert, this wasn't a big betrayal of the lads, as Nugent was simply too heavy for my prog rock, blues rock and pop rock mates. Personally I'd always fancied seeing Ted Nugent. It wasn't that I particularly liked his music, but I'd heard his shows were ear-splittingly loud and involved long, painfully drawn out guitar solos, so that was good enough for me. All I needed to do now was persuade Vivien to join me.

"Look if you're worried about the volume, I'll get us a couple of tickets in the circle and you can hardly hear it from there." She looked at me in a way that indicated she knew I was talking bullshit. I looked back at her with my sickeningly in-love, puppy-dog eyes.

"Okay, it will be a giggle," she said, smiling at me.

Too fucking right it will be a giggle, I thought to myself. *Now you're going to find out what a real rock concert is like.*

The Gig

It was post support band time and we were sitting in our rear circle seats. I could see that Vivien had really enjoyed the warm-up act (Kingfish).

"What did you think?" she asked me.

"They were good," I replied politely. In truth they had been crap, but I didn't want to dampen her enthusiasm, "And I think they will go far." Love and talking bullshit seem to go hand in hand.

"I think it would have been even better downstairs, don't you Vivien?" I hated it in the circle and having pulled off the 'downstairs scam' at the Gillan gig, I was keen to put it into practice at this one. So I explained to Vivien my tried and tested strategy for accessing the stalls.

"Isn't that illegal?" Vivien said with a worried look on her face. I guess technically we were infringing some rule by entering the stalls with a circle ticket, but to bracket it as illegal seemed a bit excessive.

"Of course not. Look, if we get caught they'll simply escort us back to our seats. It's no big deal..." I said with as much assuagement as I could pull-off. "Trust me, it's part of the concert going experience, everyone does it…" Back to bullshit mode. "If we get in and you don't like it we'll come back up here, I promise." The people in the surrounding seats moved away as the smell was becoming overpowering, but my heartfelt bullshit was starting to work, as she had a look on her face that indicated she was concerned, but excited about this 'law-breaking' activity. It was also a look that meant she was going to trust me.

"Come on, let's go to the bar and await the signal."

As we sat in the bar and talked, my mind was elsewhere. I was worried that we might get caught trying to enter the stalls and in truth, I had no idea of the consequences. I was also worried that Vivien wouldn't really like Ted Nugent and would find the whole experience just too loud and aggressive. I had this image of her standing at the back, by herself, totally pissed off, while I was at the front, arm in arm with my fellow rockers, having the time of my life. The third bell went and this time I was far more anxious than excited.

"Hold on to my shoulder, wave this ticket and we'll be fine," I said with nervous conviction.

We approached the entrance and I was really panicking now, and then, all of a sudden…we were in…phew. The lights were still on and we were standing just in front of the gents toilet. I was just confirming with Vivien that she understood the toilet part of the plan, when the lights went down, followed by an almighty cheer, followed by about half a dozen lads piling out of the gents and legging it straight down the aisle. I was just about to shout out to Vivien, not to panic, to wait and see if the crowd responded, when

165

she grabbed me by the hand and said, "Come on slow coach!"

Slow coach? Did she really just call me slow coach? I hadn't heard that term used since junior school. As we made our way to the front I was dawdling slightly, distracted by my mental note to lend Vivien my book of classic rock clichés.

As soon as Nugent blasted into the first song and the sound waves nearly blew us off our feet, Vivien was freaking out. We had a brilliant time and if I was in love before, then I was in double, double love now. She actually enjoyed Ted Nugent and was impressed by his big stack (of Marshall amps) - edit out alert. Yes, it was loud, yes it was a 90 minute guitar solo, but it was exciting and to have that wall of sound in a relatively small venue just added to the buzz.

As Nugent took his final bow I was on a massive high, not because the gig was the best ever, but because I had been both amazed and vicariously exhilarated to have witnessed Vivien's unbridled free-spirit.

Review from the Birmingham Evening Mail

The rock blast

Ted Nugent, Odeon, New Street

TED NUGENT is a musical form of grievous bodily harm.

Or, to put it another way, he would make any member of the Noise Abatement Society break down and cry.

For he is without doubt the loudest man in the world. Five minutes of Nugent and it felt like my eardrums were about to burst.

I used the term in 'music' in the loosest sense. Nugent uses his guitar like a machine gun, which spits out a succession of notes of blistering intensity.

The musical 'bullets' cascade off the walls, magnifying still further the already frightening noise.

Yet, while I was sure that brain damage was about to develop, it seemed that few, if any of the audience, were similarly worried. In fact, to my amazement, they seemed to be enjoying it all.

This adds weight to Nugent's own theory that rock music is enjoyable, but very loud rock is really exciting. By the ecstatic reaction which greeted some of Nugent's numbers, he obviously had a point.

But, having listened to his records, and found them interesting and exciting – with the volume at a normal level – surely Mr Nugent and his band would command an even bigger following if they compromised just a little.

KEN LAWRENCE

The Rock Concert Crowd

At a rock concert the crowd broadly fits into three categories:
- The out-and-out headbanger
- The head-mover
- Mr Inertia

The headbanger, the demographic group to which I fell into, displays a total unbridled connection with the music which manifests itself in having little regard for the potential brain damage such animated head movement may cause. Typically the out-and-out headbanger will only see fifty percent of the concert because half the time his head is in a downward motion towards the direction of the floor.

The head-mover has far more respect for his brain, or in certain cases has too little hair to make the headbanging ritual worthwhile. They are happy to stand up and get into the atmosphere and after the gig they are happy to fill in the half of the concert their headbanging mates have missed.

Mr Inertia is a mystery. They sit there without moving a muscle – as if it's National Rigor Mortis Day. I'm sure their connection to the music must be more subtle or internalised but they never seem to be enjoying the experience and when there is a mass wave of standing up they're always the last to rise. And then they proceed to stand there looking slightly bemused at the headbanging antics of the people around them.

Rest of 1977

As we went through the rest of 1977, we continued to ride on the back of the wonderful music scene of that period. I won tickets (on the Robin Valk show, BRMB) to see Bob Segar (*18th October 1977, Birmingham Odeon, £2.80, C27)*, an artist who ordinarily we wouldn't have bought tickets for, but who turned in an absolutely classic gig! We sat through another surreal Steve Hillage concert (*27th October 1977, Birmingham Odeon, £1.00, Rear Circle, V2)* and then legged it down the front for a great headbang to Pat Travers (*14th November 1977, Birmingham Town Hall, £1.50, Ground Floor, I20)*. Then came 'Rainbow day'(*18th November 1977, New Bingley Hall, £3.00, Ticket No.15021)* and the final gig in 1977 saw Mahogany Rush break the sound barrier, after pissing us off for an hour by coming on late. (*7th December 1977, Birmingham Town Hall, £2.00, Ground Floor, N20)*.

ODEON THEATRE
BIRMINGHAM

Harvey Goldsmith Entertainments presents
BOB SEGER and The Silver Bullet Band
Plus Support

EVENING 7-30 p.m

TUESDAY
OCTOBER **18**

FRONT STALLS
£2·80

C27

NO TICKET EXCHANGED NOR MONEY REFUNDED
THIS PORTION TO BE RETAINED   T P T O

ODEON THEATRE
BIRMINGHAM

Promotions present
STEVE HILLAGE
plus special guest GLENN PHILLIPS

EVENING 7-30 p.m.

THURSDAY
OCTOBER **27**

REAR CIRCLE
£1·00

V 2

NO TICKET EXCHANGED NOR MONEY REFUNDED
THIS PORTION TO BE RETAINED   (P.T.O.)

TOWN HALL, BIRMINGHAM

MAURICE JONES
presents

PAT TRAVERS

MONDAY, 14th NOVEMBER, 1977,
at 1930 hours

GROUND FLOOR   £1.50

PLEASE RETAIN
LATECOMERS will not be admitted until a convenient
break in the programme. Tickets cannot be exchanged or
money refunded.

Harvey Goldsmith Entertainments presents
RAINBOW
featuring RITCHIE BLACKMORE,
COZY POWELL & RONNIE JAMES DIO
plus Support

TICKET PRICE £3.00
BINGLEY HALL, STAFFORD

No re-admission
for conditions see reverse
to be retained and produced
on demand
Scot. Brm. Edn

at 7.30 pm
FRIDAY 18th
No   15021
NOVEMBER 1977

TOWN HALL, BIRMINGHAM

STRAIGHT MUSIC *presents*

MAHOGANY RUSH

WEDNESDAY, 7th DECEMBER, 1977,
at 1930 hours

GROUND FLOOR   £1.50
2·00

N 2

PLEASE RETAIN
LATECOMERS will not be admitted until a convenient
break in the programme. Tickets cannot be exchanged or
money refunded.

The lads, Oct 1977 – Age 15. From left to right: Steve; Huw (kneeling); Paul; Pete (with air guitar)

Pete: May 1978 *(age 16)*

Pete and Vivien: 1977

Huw and Vivien: 1977

PART 2

Chapter 21

The Gig Scene
(1978. Age 16)

How quickly things can change and by 1978 not only was rock *dead* but its tormentor – punk music – was also coming under fire for succumbing to the trappings of success. Well, that's what the music press were having us believe.

To me, in terms of the rock scene, nothing much had changed, rock music was still the *dog's bollocks*.

But what I will say about punk-rock is that it sounded fresh and exciting, like how rock music had sounded to me, back in 1975 – in your face and raw. It's not that I was thinking of switching musical allegiances or anything as dramatic as that, but you can't argue with the sheer in-your-face energy of the Sex Pistols or The Clash. And it's never a bad thing to have a new kid on the block come up and give you a right kick up the arse in order to help get you out of your malaise. In my heart of hearts that's how I hoped punk music would influence rock – a friendly boot up the derrière, not a fully-fledged knockout punch.

Then in 1978 I heard about a band who were going to breathe new life into rock music and specifically the heavy metal scene.

Early January 1978 – Saturday afternoon in my house with the lads.

Imagine this scenario, it's the mid-1970s. Four rock heads are planning their next move - it's going to be a ball-breaking assault on the senses; a heterosexual journey into the land of the male preserve. It's gonna be rock and it ain't gonna be pretty. *Lads, fancy going to see a gay leather-clad singer with short hair and a high voice?*

It could never have happened? Impossible in an era when there was so much terrible discrimination against homosexuality? Well, that's exactly what happened! Well not exactly what happened – it happened but we didn't know it had happened as it was happening! Confused? Let me explain. Let me introduce you to Judas Priest.

Judas Priest formed in Birmingham in 1969. By the time they started to show up on my radar they had already released three albums (*Rocka Rolla,* 1974; *Sad Wings of Destiny, 1976;* and *Sin After Sin 1977*). They were developing a unique image and musical style based around lead singer Rob Halford. Halford had an amazing operatic vocal style, as well as a more than passing interest in leather. Nothing wrong with leather as long as your leather clad body is attached to a motorbike not a bondage rack.

So the first Priest album I purchased was *Sad Wings of Destiny (based on the fact it had an amazing album cover)* which was brilliant. The songs were different. Certainly Halford's voice allowed for creative song writing but I couldn't put my finger on which classification of rock to place them in. Many decades later Priest were cited as a major influence on multiple genres of metal, including but not limited to power metal and thrash metal. But at this point in Priest's career their sound (and ultimate influence) could have gone in any number of directions.

In 1998 Rob Halford announced, what many people in the rock fraternity had always suspected, that he was gay. I always wonder with Priest – would they have been as big today if he had 'come out' in the 1970s. It shouldn't have made a difference, but I can't help thinking that sadly it would have done - homosexuality had only been decriminalised in 1967, but there were still anti-gay laws set in place and there was still widespread homophobia.

And would they have been as big today if their notoriety hadn't received a massive dose of unfortunate publicity in the form of young American kids who suddenly decided to play their albums backwards – supposedly hearing messages such as 'do it.' This led to the band being unsuccessfully sued in 1985 when two kids decided on a suicide pact after *hearing* the said subliminal message in the track *Better By You, Better By Me*. One of them died at the scene. But it was later revealed they had a violent history and one of them had attempted to choke his own mother. Tragic in every sense, but alas, after this episode Priest would gain kudos in the same way that Ozzy did for biting the head off a bat. Not kudos from the suicide, but kudos from the fact that Priest's albums took on much more of a death metal undertone. I can't say I have ever played their albums backwards and I often wonder what the stimulus was for kids to try this in the first place? In fact why bother looking for a subliminal message? You only have to listen to tracks from *Sad Wings of Destiny* or *Stained Class* (1978) - e.g. *Genocide, Ripper, Tyrant, Saints in Hell, Savage, Beyond the Realms of Death* - to find the message. It's staring you in the face! The message being........feel the metal, feel the energy, feel you belong, not that you are alone. Ultimately feel the goddamn music but please, don't take the bloody lyrics too seriously!

For what it's worth my stance on a person's sexuality is this. If Earth was invaded by an alien force (don't panic, I've not joined the Scientologists) that threatened to wipe out the human race we would (hopefully) all unite together in our fight for survival, there would be no prejudices, just a mutual need for camaraderie and trustworthiness. This is my starting point for all people of different races, culture or sexual orientation i.e. I just see the human being. Of course in reality, individual people piss me off, but that is a character flaw that cuts across the whole human race, not a particular culture or creed.

Judas Priest - 11th February 1978

(Birmingham Odeon, £1.00, Rear Circle, U21)

The connection between a band and the crowd is what defines a gig and it's what catapults a gig into the annals of classic rock history. It's hard to put your finger on exactly what creates this atmosphere. There's the obvious factors like the attitude of the band, the sound, the volume, the venue, the size of the crowd to name but a few. But ultimately there is no mathematical formula that can predict what an atmosphere is going to be like. And so it was on this Saturday night in February 1978 that the rock celestial planets weren't quite in harmony. I mean things started as normal......the lights went down, we piled out of the toilets, jogged down to the front and joined up with a good number of fellow front running rockers to take our place ahead of the expensive seats. But it wasn't a full-on assault of the stage and many rock-heads remained seated. Things didn't seem the same and for long periods of time our normal frenetic front-of-stage antics were replaced with surprising stillness. But in the end the sheer volume of the music won

through and soon we were lapping up the amazing
Judas Priest stage show.

Review from the Birmingham Evening Mail

High Priests of ear-bashing!

Judas Priest, Odeon, Birmingham

About 200 people charged to the front of the stage.

I thought the ice-cream lady had arrived. She hadn't.

All that happened was that the lights had gone out and Judas Priest had come on.

Heads waved trance like. Arms punched the air as Rob Halford launched into "Exciter" from Priest's new album "Stained Class" released last Friday.

After blasting us with "The Ripper" then "Savage" lead singer Halford asked the faithful "what's wrong with Birmingham tonight, you're very quiet?"

Well they weren't but Judas Priest would have had difficulty hearing a 21-gun salute over the racket they were making.

I turned down the offer of two pieces of cotton wool from a wise fan beside me and I moved to the back of the auditorium.

It was just as bad.

The noise level was appalling.

Disciples of the Priest loved it.

TONY McKINSTRY

So yes, Priest had been brilliant but had anything changed? Did it need to change? Did rock music really need to take heed and listen to what the punks were saying or was I just being over-sensitive? I wasn't sure. For a moment at the beginning of tonight's gig I was starting to think that the punks might have a point, but by the end of the gig I had dismissed that thought. In fact I had decided it was time to put two fingers up to the pretentious punks and show them a full on prog rock gig. Cue Rush.

Rush - 12th Feb 1978
(Birmingham Odeon, £3.00, Front Stalls, B16)

If Music Be The Food Of Love Play On.

You could hardly call Rush the new wave of rock, but they certainly weren't dinosaurs either. In fact, because they managed to fuse rock and progressive rock, the sound was fresh and exciting.

I had seen Rush the previous year on their first ever tour outside of America and Canada (*3rd June 1977, Birmingham Odeon, £1.50, Rear Circle, U47).* They played seven gigs in the UK on that tour and the third one had been a sell-out at the Odeon. Previous to this gig (early 1977), myself and Steve had gone halves on the Rush album *All the World's a Stage*, which had only been available on import. They were unknown over here at that point in time, so we went to the '77 gig not knowing what to expect. We ended up witnessing a concert that would ultimately make it into my 'top-five gigs of all time' list. So based on both mine and Steve's testimonials we had the full complement of lads and girlfriends for this gig. We had even taken the unprecedented step of paying for front stalls seats.

As we exited the Odeon, we were dripping in sweat and high on the adrenaline boost of the concert. It had been a real bonding experience with all of us locking arms for the encores.

"Didn't I tell you?" I said, as if to claim it was all my idea.

"I don't know how they manage to get that sound with only three of them in the band....it was just...." I interrupted Paul, "I know, Alex Lifeson seemed to be playing three guitars at once."

"I thought the light show was amazing as well," Vivien commented.

She was right, the light show had been amazing, and as her words drifted lazily into my conscious thoughts I looked at my girlfriend, my rock-chick and my heart hurt. As soon as the relationship had started I developed a terrible niggling insecurity that I would lose her. It's a stark counterweight to the highs of being in love. In truth, when she touched the tips of my rock-loser fingers in the Stourbridge Swimming baths back on July 15th 1977, it was as if some greater force had touched me and suddenly brought me to life. Rock music had given me a meaning in life, an identity, a spirit, but Vivien took me to the apogee of human emotions. But with such a gift of internal exaltation comes responsibility and unfortunately my ability to garnish such intense feelings of love was sadly lacking. I knew Vivien loved me intently but I often felt her feelings were controlled by her mind not her heart.

For me, there was no compromise, there was no controlling cognitive function – it was 100% heartfelt.

Fortunately at this stage in our relationship the highs still significantly outweighed the lows.

Review from the Birmingham Evening Mail

Rush of excitement to the brain

Rush, Odeon, New Street, Birmingham

For a Canadian band, Rush play pretty good British rock music.

They could, in fact, be a heavier version of British supergroups like Yes and Genesis. Yet Rush are no 3-man copycat act.

They are merely more sophisticated and thoughtful about their music than the great majority of heavy rock bands from across the Atlantic. Most of those are too brash and gimmicky for British audiences.

Rush, in fact, appeared to be just another loud rock band on their last visit here. But they have developed into a highly stylised, exciting group who, though obviously influenced by Yes and Genesis, are breaking new ground for themselves.

Neil Peart (drums), Geddy Lee (bass), Alex Lifeson (lead guitar) are still relatively unknown in Britain. But last night's excellent performance, with a tremendous light show to add extra atmosphere, had the sell-out audience on their feet throughout.

Their music was fast, pulsating and, above all, memorable.

KEN LAWRENCE

There is absolutely no doubt that Rush were awesome and had it been the mid-70s there would have been no negatives to be found whatsoever. But that night, when I was lying awake in bed the doubts came flooding back and I couldn't help feeling that rock was crying out for a sound that would take it back to basics, a sound that could counter what the punks had said about rock. I don't know who I was talking to, but in my head I just kept saying *'let there be rock, let there be rock.'*

Monty Python

Almost as big an influence on our sub-culture at that time and certainly a huge influence on our sentence construction were the works of Monty Python's Flying Circus. Our observations, ripostes and punch lines were littered with Python references. Why Monty Python? Well I guess it was because Python's comedy represented and paralleled the sense of freedom (from the shackles of what was considered convention) that was a prime feature of rock music. If you take the view point that Python were the icons of satire and Led Zeppelin the icons of rock, well both came on the scene at the same time: Led Zeppelin's first album 1969; the first episode of Python 1969. Python also stretched the limits of acceptability, just like rock music. Think of Sabbath and the occult and Python and religion, yet both of these connections were analogous and were not meant to be taken seriously.

The link was also made through the 'Secret Policeman' benefits shows for Amnesty International, in which rock(*ish*) acts and comedians joined together on stage. That's why Monty Python had such a big influence on our sub-culture.

Also, Python's humour was so off-the-wall that on the whole most people didn't get it - it wasn't mainstream (just like rock music wasn't mainstream). But of course, it didn't matter if we didn't get it, the most important thing was never letting on that we didn't get it...and then never letting on why it was important to never let on that we didn't get it. The whole charade made perfect sense.

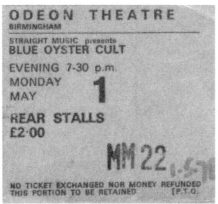

Blue Oyster Cult (BOC) - 1st May 1978
(Birmingham Odeon, £2.00, Rear Stalls, MM22)

This was one of those nights when everything clicked. If punks had been present, they may have scoffed at the drum solo; whinged at the over-the-top light show; gobbed at the extended guitar solos; ridiculed the 20 minute rendition of *Don't Fear the Reaper*; derided the slightly large bouffants; and mocked the rather bizarre lyrics - but apart from the drum solos, guitar solos, long-drawn out tracks, big hair, and meaningless lyrics, I think Blue Oyster Cult had shown the punk-rockers that rock was going nowhere. Or at least that it was going nowhere fast.

Review from the Birmingham Evening Mail

Light fantastic – and music too!

Blues Oyster Cult, Odeon, Birmingham.
SO FAR, 1978 has been the year of the light show.
Nowadays, it is not enough just to play the music –
there has to be a visual side to the entertainment.
Last night's Blue Oyster Cult show was the best I've
seen yet. At times the stage resembled the mothership
from "Close Encounters," and throughout the evening
vivid laser lights arrowed around the hall.
Their brand of rock'n'roll is not for the faint hearted.
This five-piece New York group let us have it at breath-
taking pace right from the start, and didn't let up until
the final crescendo, a glorious rendering of the classic
"Born To Be Wild."
But this was anything but the only high spot. When
Albert Bouchard was left on stage with his drums,
another boring solo seemed imminent. Instead the
next 10 minutes was amazing with laser lights now
swirling through the audience.
And the rest of the band returned to finish off "Godzilla"
in champion style.
Blue Oyster Cult are like a grittier yet more
sophisticated version of Status Quo. While enjoying
supergroup status in America their following in Britain
is still growing.

KEN LAWRENCE

Chapter 22

Growing Up
(1978: First Job)

1978 was 'O-level' year and whilst the lads and Vivien all headed off to Sixth Form College to continue their education and follow their identified career path, I searched for a job down the road of non-direction.

O-level results identified a big difference in academic achievement between me and the friends around me and when something makes you start to question yourself or your own behaviour it invariably creates an uncomfortable feeling. To me, the meaning of life was rock music, my mates and my girlfriend. But my internal questioning made me start to wonder whether my whole life was just a charade? Was I living in a bubble that could burst at any moment? This was the first time I'd taken my head out of the sand for a long time and it wasn't a pleasant experience. So I quickly stuck it straight back in again.

My lack of dedication to academia was rewarded with the high octane rock'n'roll job of clerical assistant at the Birmingham Rates Office and in September 1978 I reported for duty at 120 Edmund Street, Birmingham.

There were many people who worked at the Rates Office: male, female, old, young, black, white, but not one...not one fellow rocker. In the team I was

191

assigned to worked a bloke called Tom. He was a year older than me and had been there for nearly 12 months. Tom was a soul-boy, with soul-boy clothes and a soul-boy haircut. I was the new boy, with new boy clothes and loser boy haircut. I made an easy target and it wasn't long before the piss-takes and the put-downs were sent to test my resolve. I was a 16 year-old rocker starting my first job and ripe for a bit of new-boy humiliation. In addition, the whole culture made me feel uncomfortable. People talked about strange subjects like families, soap operas and what they did the previous evening, oh and more often than not other work colleagues (behind their back). If ever I tried to inject a bit of satirical humour into the conversation I received a look that said "what the bloody-hell is this cheese-dick talking about." It was not a happy first few weeks. I was a fish out of water and it would have been easy to retreat into my shell and continue to rely on the social crutch of the lads back home and the emotional support of Vivien. But I thought of the words my father used to say to me; he said *'Son, you're a waste of space,'* and then I remembered the other words he used to say; he said *'Son, always stand up for yourself.....especially against soul-boys.'* Okay, I admit, I made the soul-boy bit up, but he was right, you can't just run away from your troubles otherwise you'll always be running and besides, rockers never ever run away from soul-boys. Well, almost never.

So I stood up for myself and very soon I was part of the Rates Office drinking clique. It's a sad fact of life that if you are meek and mild there is a high probability that people will take advantage of you. Being assertive means you get to drink shed loads with fellow piss-heads.

At home, drink had steadily been making its way up our social agenda. And visits to our local pub - the Swan in Old Swinford were becoming the norm. But alcohol was still only an add-on, not a key part of the evening. Starting work at the Rates Office upped the drinking ante significantly.

The traditional first pub stop for the Rates Office Thursday drinking clique was the Gaiety, yes the Gaiety and no it wasn't (it is now called The Roebuck). There were five of, what I presumed to be, the regular crowd there for my initiation ceremony, all older than me. Other than Tom, I had never spoken to any of them. I had only passed them in the office so Tom introduced me to them. This was not a harmonious situation for me, so I sat there in mute mode trying to work out something witty to add to the conversation that wasn't going to be a Monty Python quote. Five pints of Skol lager later and I was trading ground strokes with the banter merchants and actually starting to feel comfortable with a group of non-rock-heads. For the first time that I can remember alcohol had served a purpose other than adding the icing to a great night out – it gave me confidence.

It was a memorable first evening in as much that, I could hardly remember any of it! And soon the Thursday night club would become an integral part of my week.

Rock was crying out for a sound that would take it back to basics, a sound that could counter what the punks had said about rock. I don't know who I was talking to, but in my head I just kept saying 'let there be rock, let there be rock.'

Chapter 23

The Gig Scene
(1978 Continued)

Let There be Rock

I'd heard a track on the radio by a little known Aussie band that were making a name for themselves. Although the track didn't have the same magnitude as my *Deep Purple in Rock* or *Freebird* moments, it wasn't far off. In 1974 and 1975 the Purple and Skynyrd tracks had lit a huge bonfire inside of me, but now, three years later, the flames needed stoking and AC/DC had just stuck a red hot poker into my fire. I was off to buy *Let There Be Rock*. Three minutes and six seconds of sheer high-octane energy. When I got back I played it over and over again. I absolutely loved it. I still do.

AC/DC - 9th Nov 1978

(Birmingham Odeon, £1.80, Rear Stalls, NN38)

AC/DC had been touring for a while with the likes of Black Sabbath and Back Street Crawler but this was one of their first tours as the headline act. The gig had everything and attracted both old guard rockers and new rockers.

Having started going to concerts aged 14 and having turned 17 two days earlier I should have been sitting there all cool and calm and in control of my emotions. Instead I was so racked with nerves of anticipation that I was reeling off the *'Wally'* cries like he was actually missing.

The lights hadn't gone down but a cheer went up in the crowd. I didn't see what happened but before I could say 'school boy error' a herd of rockers swept majestically down the aisle, man and hair in perfect harmony. Soon it was 'security guard and rookie rocker in perfect harmony' as the excitable youngsters were marched back to their seats. I smiled to myself as I remembered that earlier this year I had done exactly the same thing, only more embarrassingly. Steve and I had become a bit too confident when it

196

came to leading a charge to the front and at a Rory Gallagher gig we suddenly found ourselves totally isolated. Not a sausage, not one rocker joined us and when we ran into the wall that was the front stall bouncers they politely suggested that we reconsider our plans. As we retreated we bowed our heads in a vain attempt to hide our rock loser tattoos that were now branded on our foreheads, but the crowd were beside themselves with ironic applause. Fellow rockers can be a cruel bunch when they get going.

Whatever the outcome, running to the front was part of the rock culture of the time and if you were part of it, it was a real thrill. Admittedly in the greater scheme of things that may sound a sad way to get ones thrills, but when you're charging forward like General Custer, leading your troops into battle, it's a real adrenaline rush.

Anyway, back to the gig. Soon the lights went down and the same herd of rockers that had passed me 10 minutes earlier came storming back down with little regard for the seating instructions previously given to them by the bouncers. This time we joined the back of them and found a good place to stand just off the main pack on the cusp of row D. From the first power chord of the first number it was headbanging heaven. We weren't there to be dazzled by technical musical wizardry, no, we wanted it loud, down to earth and we wanted a show. I had seen too many rock bands rely on fancy lighting or instrumental solos to pull their gig through. What we really craved for were bands to be genuine and feel as much passion for what they were playing as we felt in the crowd. We wanted a connection and with AC/DC, they went straight for the balls.

About an hour into the concert the band played the mighty *Rocker* and they were about three minutes into the song when Bon Scott (lead singer) and Angus Young (lead guitarist) left the stage.

"Where have they gone?" I shouted to Vivien, headbanging induced sweat pouring from my brow. She shrugged her shoulders and my sweat turned cold at the thought of an impending drum and bass solo. Then suddenly we could hear Angus's guitar, but no Angus. Then there was a big roar behind us, up in the balcony. Crikey! There he was on Bon Scott's shoulders. In rock loser fashion I pointed to the circle to a sight that nobody could have missed. This was just brilliant, fantastic, out of this world. They disappeared again and we were left standing there open mouthed. Then they reappeared at the back of the stalls. I pointed again as they made their way down the middle of the aisle; all this time the band continued playing *Rocker* on stage as Angus continued to play lead guitar whilst remaining on Bon Scott's shoulders.

I was orgasmic with excitement. This was what a rock concert was all about. And as the song came to its climax I really thought I was going to join it. Apologies…I'm getting carried away with the memory.

If you get chance, have a look at the YouTube video: '*AC/DC – Rocker [Colchester, England, 10/28/1978].*' Watching it sends shivers down my spine, knowing how amazing it was to have witnessed this great spectacle.

As the band left the stage they got a huge reception and very soon they were back on for their first encore. Angus banged out the power chords to *Whole Lotta Rosie* and between the power chords we shouted out Angus's name, as if we had been programmed to do so from birth. Then Bon sang:

"42-39-56......You could say she's got it all"

Everyone - and I mean everyone - just went crazy; it was wondrous, joyous mayhem. I'd never seen a rock group galvanise a crowd like this before. Yes, groups had created unbelievable reactions from fans but never on this scale. What rubbed off on the crowd the most was the band really did look like they were enjoying it. AC/DC had just raised the bar for live performances and boy had they raised it high.

"This is the best ever, nothing will ever top this," I shouted to Vivien as the encore was coming to an end. I'd said it after Be-Bop Deluxe, I'd said it after Rainbow and I'd said it after Lynyrd Skynyrd, but this time the exclamation would never be repeated (see 'Top Five Gigs of All Time' list – next page).

I have one simple word to sum up the concert.....

......*mindblowingearthshatteringwhiskysnortingsound breakingheadbangingsolidrockgogogoch*

Review from the Birmingham Evening Mail

Electric shock to the senses

AC/DC, Odeon, Birmingham.
I almost drove past the Odeon this morning….just to see if it was still standing.

Last night it was subjected to such a violent assault of noise, it could well have been reduced to a pile of rubble.

AC/DC brought their brand of high voltage rock to the home of heavy metal….the same Midlands that produced Led Zeppelin and Black Sabbath. So to win over such an audience this Aussie five-piece had better be darn good.

Testimony to that was a chanting crowd near hysteria long before the band started to pulverise the eardrums As the lights went down, a mass surge took thousands to the front, to girate frantically in time with the pulsating drums of Phill Rudd and the perfectly in-step bass of Cliff Williams.

Outfront singer Bon Scott screaches inaudible vocals into the mike while the crowd's hero, lead guitarist Angus Young, thrashes around the stage, demented.

Their style is way out of date, Zeppelin were doing this years ago, but the crowd – and I say crowd because it looked more like the Holte End than a concert audience – were not bothered with the finer points….they were there to have their senses smashed with the most powerful rock band I have heard.

Paul Walker.

AC/DC became one of the most successful hard rock bands of all time. In its own way, it was rock's reaction against itself, against what the punks had called the pompous and lumbering arena rock of the '70s. AC/DC had taken rock music back to basics. I was a happy rocker: *Let There Be Rock!*

My Top Five Gigs of All Time
1. *AC/DC, 9th Nov 1978, Birmingham Odeon*
2. *Lynyrd Skynyrd, 2nd Feb 1977, Birmingham Odeon*
3. *Rainbow, 11th Sept 1976, Birmingham Odeon*
4. *Rush, 3rd June 1977, Birmingham Odeon*
5. *Rory Gallagher, 21st April 1978, Birmingham Odeon*

Why AC/DC at Number 1?
What I look for in a concert is a band that wants to entertain the crowd, not just play to the crowd. Ultimately a rock concert comes under the umbrella of the Entertainment Industry and therein there should be an inherent desire by a band to put on a show. That doesn't necessarily mean spending thousands of pounds on lighting, lasers, pyrotechnics and other visual paraphernalia, but it's more about trying to make a connection with the audience. And the root of that connection is how the band behave on stage. If they look like they are there purely for financial reasons or if you can sense friction in the band or if they look washed up through too much touring, alcohol or drugs then this vibe is passed onto the audience

and that special connection between musicians and the fans is lost.

AC/DC, especially in the Bon Scott era had *joie de vivre* in bucket loads. They looked like they were having an absolute ball. Like they knew and appreciated how lucky they were to be living the rock'n'roll dream. And to add the icing onto the cake they put so much energy into their show that it was just an amazing spectacle. And to add the icing onto the icing, they were playing relatively small venues like the Birmingham Odeon where you could stand right up against the stage and see every nuance of their performance.

Lynyrd Skynyrd came a close second to AC/DC (re my top five gigs of all time) and it's no coincidence that in Ronnie Van Zant and Bon Scott they had two of the most charismatic front men in rock music.

Headbanging For Dummies

If you have never been to a rock gig it may be hard for you to understand the level of connection with the music. You may find it perplexing why rockers choose to represent this connection in the form of headbanging and general front-of-stage mayhem.

Well, especially for those of you who are rock music virgins, I'm going to take you through a step by step headbanging guide on how to behave if you unexpectedly find yourself in the heaving front-of-stage mass. This is an important lesson, because when you're in a tight knit band of rockers you need to be confident that those around you know what to do and aren't suddenly going to panic and bring chaos to the well-ordered mayhem.

Firstly, whenever the lead guitarist plays a solo, then this is an appropriate time to raise both hands in the air and give a 'V' sign. Make sure your palms are facing forward as you don't want to offend the fragile egos of the band members.

Alternatively if it's a full moon you can give the sign of the horns which requires your hand to extend the index and little fingers while holding the middle and ring fingers down with the thumb. This sign was popularized by Ronnie James Dio, although Black Sabbath's Geezer Butler was raising his horn as far back as 1971.

When the rhythm section takes over keep your hands in the air and build up a steady headbanging motion. Nothing too extravagant, as you're just keeping in time with the music.

Don't be afraid to exaggerate the movement of your air guitar strumming hand, to indicate you're fully familiar with the technicalities of a song's subtle arrangement.

It's not so important to sing along to a verse because in most rock songs nobody has a clue what the lead vocalist is actually singing about, but mumbling your interpretation of what you think they are singing is perfectly acceptable.

Be sure to keep your cool and listen carefully for any explosions of tempo that require a more free and random leaping up and down movement. For the more ambidextrous amongst you, the maintenance of the headbanging cadence while simultaneously leaping up and down will gain you extra credibility at a gig. And watch out for the potential to leap on the shoulder of the person in front of you. And don't be alarmed if your shoulder also becomes a launch pad for the person behind you. It's not always guaranteed and will depend on how pissed everyone is. If all is going according to plan then you will be in perfect harmony with your fellow rockers and the front-of-stage mass will look like one finely tuned headbanging machine.

When a guitar solo includes a couple of high notes or big bends be sure to arch your back and tilt your head backwards and express the ecstasy of these moments. But don't overdo it and reverse head-butt the person behind you as this may result in the said person giving unwanted reconstruction surgery to your nasal area.

If the song moves back into a slightly quieter phase, it's time to put both your hands back in the air and salute the band. Whatever you do, don't just stand there as you will look a total twat, or worse still, fellow rockers will think you don't like the music and…..you've guessed it…….the hooter cops it again.

If a song speeds up at the end – known as accelerando – you are free to express your headbanging expertise in any way that grabs your fancy. This is no time to consult your notes. This is what rock music is all about. It's the sheer adrenaline rush as the song moves you into a different world. Shout out the words…scream out the words (or at least your interpretation of the words) and get down on your knees to the guitar solo. As the end of the song approaches, put your hands back in the air and applaud the final note.

Well done, you are now a fully qualified headbanger.

****

Of course, to a rational person this sort of behaviour may look a bit odd. They may think they have stumbled on some experiment to prove that Darwin's theory was right. They may conclude that the experiment is at the Ape Man point in the evolutionary cycle, with the primates now able to leap about, grunt and place their arms in the air-guitar position. But, hey, who cares…we having fun.

And remember, for those about to rock…we salute you.

On 20th December 1979, I saw AC/DC for the final time with Bon Scott as their front man (Birmingham Odeon, £3.75, Front Stalls, D14). For this gig, behind the drummer, they'd created a platform on top of the Marshall stacks. A duck-walking paradise for Angus. And for reasons unknown the gig also featured two exotic dancers. Or to be more accurate, strippers, who also took full advantage of the platform on top of the Marhall amps. They came on during AC/DC's classic song *The Jack* (also known as *She's got the Jack*). And, as far as I could make out they tried their best to perform some carefully choreographed movements, creating a sense of beauty against the song's subtle melody. However I got the feeling that this may have been lost a tad during a song that is about venereal disease. But hey, at least they tried. And at the end of the song their efforts did not go unappreciated amongst the highly knowledgeable and culturally erect male dominated crowd.

Homage to Bon

Sadly, 61 days after the strippers gig, Bon was dead. By this time Bon Scott was a legend amongst the ever growing legion of AC/DC fans. He seemed like a lads' man, one who liked a wild time but always seemed to do it with a cheeky grin. We, the fans, loved that but sadly Bon died on February 19th 1980 when, after a night of heavy drinking, he choked to death on his own vomit. It was a tragedy. After much soul searching AC/DC decided to continue on and eventually found a replacement for Bon, in Brian Johnson.

****

I remember on one of our holidays we found Huw asleep in his tent after a heavy night of drinking and he was making the most awful sound. We could see that he was trying to vomit even though he was asleep. We moved him on to his side and left him to it. Thankfully he didn't roll back on to his back, because at that young age we had no idea that it could have resulted in his death. In the morning the vomit was on his sleeping bag. Had someone found Bon we might still be saluting him today but, like all icons that die young, his image is now cemented in stone and will live on forever.

Let there be rock.

Chapter 24

Growing Up
(1978: Disco)

What Is A Twain? And What's It Got To Do With Rockers And Discos?

Back at the Rates Office I was a well-established member of the Thursday drinking club. Drinking brought us together and drinking was our bond. We were there to have uncomplicated fun and in December 1978 that fun started to extend out of the pubs and into the night clubs.

I hate night clubs.

It's important to understand that with rock music the headbanging beat requires no utilisation of the lower limbs, other than for stability. Therefore when the rocker finds himself in the alien world of the night club the first thing he does is seek out the bar - to drink the beer that starts to refresh the parts that sobriety can't reach. So after eight pints and with my senses fully numbed I would make the fatal error of concluding that my complete lack of rhythm had been miraculously cured. And, when, on to the turntable came *Night Fever* or *You're The One That I Want* I would strut around the dance floor like...well, like a pissed up rocker. Not an aesthetically pleasing sight.

As the weekly Thursday night disco *fun* continued, I quickly learned that I needed to separate upper and lower body activity in order to at least create some

208

semblance of rhythmic (not robotic) movement. So after careful consideration of the bio-mechanics of the disco dancing movement, I decided to adopt a fixed lower frame position from which the upper body could flow. However my lack of lower limb movement made for an interesting dance floor spectacle that soon afforded me the tag of disco dummy. But hey, it was all good drunken fun. Ultimately it reinforced what I already knew: rockers are rockers, discos are discos and never the twain shall meet.

When we did sit down to talk, the conversation rarely strayed outside our comfort zones and a whole evening out drinking would be spent talking about last week's drinking or infamous tales of drinking. Occasionally the subject matter was interrupted by a debate on whose turn it was to buy the next round; but then it quickly returned to more tales of drinking, the content of which became more exaggerated as the evening wore on.

I have to say I enjoyed it immensely; it was always a good laugh, never leery and basically in its own uncomplicated way, it had its own sense of freedom. For a bunch of non-rockers, those lads were brilliant.

Chapter 25

The Gig Scene
(1979)

1979 brought a year of change. Musically I was diversifying and I was starting to spend my lunch hours in Reddington's Rare Records (RRR). The shop was in Digbeth just on the outskirts of Birmingham City Centre. It seemed like it was hidden away from the mainstream shopping area, just like rock music seemed hidden away from mainstream culture. They had absolutely everything; it was like an Aladdin's cave of rock treasure. They would always have loud music blasting away in the shop and the only depressing thing was that most of the time I'd never heard the track. I'd enquire as to the name of the band and before I knew it I was buying the damn thing. I started to get into bands that had been around for quite a while, but were still relatively unknown to the majority of mainstream rockers. Bands like Pink Fairies, Taste, MC5, Godz, Iron Butterfly, Atomic Rooster. Plus new bands such as Riot, Gamma (formed by guitarist Ronnie Montrose) and Pavlov's Dog, whose album I started salivating over (okay, I didn't really but come on, it was too good a pun to miss). My fetish for Southern American Rock also led me to the Outlaws, The Marshall Tucker Band, Blackfoot, 38 Special and Molly Hatchet.

George Thorogood & the Destroyers - 10th March 1979
(Leicester University)

Bad To The Bone

One day whilst listening to John Peel he played a track that really made me sit up and take notice. I recall *Peely* saying that the guy sure knew how to play the guitar. The next day I remember thinking that at last I could get one over on those know-alls at RRR, by asking for an album that I was convinced they wouldn't have heard of. So at lunchtime I rushed down to the shop and with a cocky voice shouted out over the loud music "I don't suppose you have the album *Move It On Over* by George Thorogood and the Destroyers do you?" I supported my cocky voice with a cocky look and was waiting for the assistant to grab a piece of paper to note down the name of this little known artist.

"Do you mean the album that we are playing in the shop right now?" he said with crushing sarcasm. I felt about 3 feet tall and walked out the shop vowing never to return. But of course I did and I did buy the album as well. An all too familiar tale of addiction.

When I got home I went straight to the track I'd heard on the radio, George Thorogood's classic version of Chuck Berry's *It Wasn't Me*. I played it until the needle bled and very soon I had learnt every note of the solo on my air guitar. I knew his high-energy blues style would be right up Steve's street and sure enough he was an immediate convert. When I found

211

out George Thorogood was touring, we snapped up tickets at the nearest venue, Leicester University.

The Gig

One Bourbon, One Scotch, One Beer

"Hey, Leicester, are you ready to boogie all night long?" George asked us (the audience) after the third number. We gave George a loud and lucid affirmative to his question.

"I said, are you ready to boogie all night long?" George repeated with slightly more passion. We gave the same affirmative reply, but with even more gusto.

"I said, are you ready to boogie all night long?"

What is he? Bloody deaf or something? I couldn't help but say to myself. Maybe he was a bit mutton from having stood in front of all those Marshall amps for all those years, or maybe my sarcastic inner thoughts were the first sign that I was tiring of the bullshit. I quickly snapped out of it and for the third time we, the crowd, grunted a big loud YES! Finally, George was satisfied that we wanted to boogie all night long and at 10.30pm he buggered off stage never to be seen again. George was raw, George was loud and George was direct, but he wasn't one for a late night. *Just the one beer please.*

George Thorogood has now sold over 15 million albums worldwide.

Rock Music And The Image – Part 2

The thing about George Thorogood was that, if anything, he had seemed too nice. There is nothing wrong with our rock heroes wanting to be jolly nice chaps, so long as they do it quietly. Our rock gods are meant to be the upholders of our unrequited dreams. We are investing our hard earned cash in our favourite bands so they will take us away from our daily grind. Normal behaviour is simply not acceptable and in order to get our vicarious fix it is essential that they live life to the full. The last thing we want to hear is that they go to bed early and drink Horlicks. They are our elected representatives of the free spirit; mischievous but not malevolent; unacceptable but within *acceptable* limits; over the top but not through the roof; excessive but not destructive.

Alas, some of them died far too young. I guess there is a fine line between good old fashioned free spirited excess and the much darker free spirited self-destruction. Speaking as a fan, these were very sad moments in rock's history and for a while it reminds you that there *is* a flip side to the unremitting hedonism. But, very soon, in order not to let these tragedies spoil the myth, we place our fallen heroes, like Bon Scott, on a pedestal and eulogise that they died while living the dream.

A Poem To Our Departed Rock Heroes

This is a eulogy
To our departed rock greats
They gave life to our lives
And in us their memory survives

With each one that leaves us
We feel the loss
Janis Joplin, Jim Morrison
And the wonderful Koss

Keith Moon, oh he gave the skins
Such a 'welly'
And never failed, after each gig,
To lob out the telly

If hell-raising was a sport
Bon Scot won by a mile
He made it look such good fun
With his innocent, cheeky smile

On the drums
John Bonham, he had few peers
To the joy he gave
I raise a glass.....cheers!

Phil Lynott of Thin Lizzy
His great songs live on
The 'Boy will always be in Town'
Departed but not gone

In Southern America
Ronnie Van Zant was first heard
Until tragedy in 1977
Now he is 'free as a bird'

And last but not least
The man who stood tall
James Marshall Hendrix
The greatest of them all

This is a eulogy
To our departed rock greats
They gave life to our lives
And in us their memory survives

1979: Rockers v Mods

The conflict between mods and rockers has its roots in the British youth subculture of the early to mid-1960s. The subculture of the rocker was centred around motorbikes, leather jackets and a big-it-up pompadour hairstyle. The rocker in this sense of the word was more associated with 1950s rock and roll — not heavy rock music. Mods wore suits, rode scooters and preferred music genres such as soul, ska and beat music. So it was, that if you put two groups of young lads in the same room and they looked different, dressed differently and were affiliated to a totally different sub-culture then there was a high probability that they wouldn't engage in a game of Twister. Instead, they would choose to celebrate their differences in the time honoured fashion of a mass brawl. Such was the hysteria surrounding this cultural disagreement that the media thought it their moral duty to denigrate such anti-social behaviour, with the Birmingham Post (May 1964), declaring that mods and rockers were "internal enemies" in the UK who would "bring about disintegration of a nation's character."

So the conflict was between young adults into 1950s rock and roll and those into soul, ska and beat music. This had nothing to do with young adults into classic rock - other than we looked different, dressed differently and were affiliated to a totally different sub-culture.

Rockers v Skinheads

We never went looking for any trouble. We weren't like that. Why was it then that we found ourselves staring down the barrel of a room full of skinheads eager to demonstrate their disapproval of our perceived mocking of their music. Well, this is what happened......

The Barmouth Trip

One weekend in 1979 the lads and I decided to take a trip to Barmouth in Wales. It was a Saturday and that evening there was a disco on at a community venue in the centre of the resort. We thought we would go along because basically there was sod all else to do.

"This is not good." We had entered the disco and I was speaking without moving my lips. This was a strange decision as all of the soul-boys who were now looking directly at us could hear fine, but I'm pretty sure they could not read lips.

"Look confident." Paul continued the ventriloquist act. Being the pop-rocker and therefore by association, being the closest thing to a soul-boy, Paul took on the role of leader. Without any further exchange of words we followed him to the bar. Subconsciously we were all walking with a bit more of a swagger. If this had been a Hollywood movie, we would have been shouting out "We're bad, we're bad mother-fuckers, we're bad..." However, this was a disco in Barmouth and an element of tact was required. We had entered enemy territory and we needed to bed in and hold our ground. Paul ordered a round and the soul-boys carried on dancing and we started to relax a little. A quick 180 degree visual sweep of the terrain revealed very little in the way of Welsh tottie.

"Shall we neck these and leg it?" Huw's question seemed to make perfect sense.

"Oh, come on lads, we've paid to get in, let's at least stay for a couple of beers." Paul's legs were already tapping out the disco beat.

"Okay, but let's get this shit off and get some decent music on." I denigrated the soul-boys musical tastes with confidence, as I knew they were out of ear shot. "Paul, go and ask for some decent shit."

Disco DJs in the late '70s and early '80s seemed to carry around the same rock singles, as if they were all given an emergency glass box when they graduated from their DJ school. The box would come with a small hammer, with the words 'Break glass only if rock-heads enter disco.' In the box the DJ would find:

- Free: *All Right Now*
- Status Quo: *Down, Down*
- Deep Purple: *Smoke on the Water*

Sure enough on came *All Right Now* and we gathered in a circle and banged our united heads until the final bars of the third track - *Smoke on the Water* - came to an end. And then it returned to soul music and we retreated back to the bar. By this time we'd had a couple of lagers and we were starting to become a bit

219

more animated towards our skin-head dancing *friends*. Finally, Paul could no longer suppress his pop inclinations and started to dance, which we found most amusing.

So this was the scenario: we had entered a soul-boy disco dressed in our denims. We had asked for some rock to be played and got up and headbanged. Then, when the soul music returned we laughed out loud when one of our number started to dance around. If, before we'd entered the disco, one of us had tabled such a motion, the word "suicide" may have been used as a response to such a suggestion. Yet, this is exactly what we did and it didn't take long before the soul-boys stopped dancing and, instead, huddled together. After what must have been some intense brainstorming, they decided that the best response to our perceived mockery was to resort to the nostalgic and much loved punch-up.

The entire venue seemed to suddenly turn on the four of us and at that moment I once again remembered the words my father used to say to me: *'Son, always stand up for yourself.'* But this was no time for fancy sound-bites. Diplomacy was called for. So we tried to reason with them that sociologically speaking we were rockers not rock'n'rollers and we existed independently of that sub-culture and therefore they were getting their danders all in a fluster over nothing. But they didn't seem to care about human social behaviour, patterns of social relationships, social interaction, and aspects of culture associated with everyday life. Instead they just stared at us blankly.

And so this is what *could* have happened next:

A mass brawl started; fists were flying everywhere; tables and chairs were flying everywhere. And general chaos was everywhere. Everyone was having fun beating each other up. We were outnumbered but we held our own. Then the mayhem ended. It had been a fight scene right out of a cowboy movie. No one had got hurt – just a few cuts and bruises. And now there was a mutual respect. And we spent the rest of the evening laughing about the brawl and chilling out together.

Yes, it could have happened like that, but instead, we legged it out the door.

They've buggered off.
So they have. They've scarpered

They ran away.
("No!")
They ran away.
("We didn't!")
When danger reared its ugly head,
They bravely turned their tails and fled.
("We never!")

© *Monty Python and the Holy Grail*

Chapter 26

The Gig Scene
(1979 Continued)

Thin Lizzy - 10th April 1979
(Stafford New Bingley Hall)

The 'Five Cheers' Gig

I took Vivien, Paul and Paul's newly acquired girlfriend Mandy on the road to see Lizzy. So we set off at 4.30pm for what was becoming a pain of a journey to get to the New Bingley Hall, Stafford.

We eventually arrived at 6.40p.m and we were greeted by torrential rain and an almighty queue to get in. "It's never like this at the Odeon," I said apologetically, as if, because I was the driver and the ticket purchaser, I was somehow to blame.

"Don't worry," said Vivien, "it looks like the weather is clearing up and the wait will give us a chance to get some food." It was a perfect synopsis of the situation and it relieved my rising frustration. The raw burgers we purchased ensured my frustration returned with interest and the burgers were duly reunited with the dog shite they had clearly been made from. But our spirits were lifted again when, the rain did indeed stop and we could appreciate a warm end to the day. In fact it warmed up so much that after much consultation and deliberation, it was decided that I should take our coats back to the car. True, this in itself is not a particularly interesting fact, but there is a point to me mentioning it. Finally at about 7.30pm we were nearing the entrance.

"Might as well give us our tickets now," said Paul.

"No problem," I said, blissfully ignorant of the impending doom.

Wearing just jeans and a Rainbow concert t-shirt, it quickly became apparent that the tickets were not on my person. This was Paul's girlfriend's first gig and having endured a two hour car journey, a soaking, a one hour queue, a raw burger and endless stories of how much fun the concert-going experience is, the last thing she needed to hear was that I had forgotten the tickets.

"I've forgotten the tickets!" I said in a state of dysfunctional panic.

"Don't be silly." Vivien always saw sense when all around was confusion. "You definitely had them when we set off. You showed them to me."

"The coats!" shouted out Paul, as if he'd just got a full-house at bingo.

I had joined all the dots and was legging it back to the car. Sure enough the tickets were in the coat that half an hour earlier I had been wearing in the queue. As I was running back to Vivien and the others I kept thinking that I'd cocked up and so I desperately wanted to restore some pride. I needed to say or do something that would re-build my perceived status as a cool rock dude.

It happened so quickly that there was nothing I could do. I was running *majestically* across the grass to the coordinates that my mental navigational system had set re the location of Viv and the others. Unfortunately the system was faulty and the coordinates hadn't taken into account queue movement and on receiving hand waving signals to indicate I was off course I took the necessary corrective action and coolly shifted direction to the right. The force of my sidestep, when transferred into the underlying muddy grass, meant that instead of the movement resulting in a balletic change of direction, I went arse over tit. I landed spread eagled in the mud, right in front of the long queue of people. This resulted in the fifth biggest cheer of the evening and my credentials as a cool rock head were well and truly in tatters. I took a bow to the cheering crowd, as if to indicate that I'd intended to fall over, but I don't think they bought it. When I reached Vivien and the others, there was little counselling on offer for my shattered self-esteem and the act of handing over the mud covered tickets just increased the levity.

.

10 minutes later

"Hey, swamp thing...what do you know about the support band?" Paul knew how to milk a moment. But his question presented me with a chance to restore some pride. I had read a review on the support band the week before.

"They're called the Vipers and I think they're going to be shit hot. I heard a track of theirs on the radio the other day (I hadn't) and it was the business. Punk'ish, but really good, they could even give Lizzy a run for their money. In fact, I think I read somewhere that they did one of the John Peel sessions. This crowd are going to love 'em."

My disciples looked impressed and I was starting to feel more like a well-oiled rock head, rather than a rock version of Frank Spencer. Events had turned around and now it was going to be a good evening. What could possibly go wrong? The lights went down and the Vipers came on stage.

Two minutes later the Vipers walked off stage.

I should have known better than to sing the praises of a support band, especially when in truth I'd heard nothing of their repertoire. I should also have instinctively known that the crowd were pissed off for having to queue to get in the car park, queue to get in the arena and be subject to raw burgers and torrential rain. They were not a bunch of happy rockers and somebody was going to pay: on came the Vipers. (The Vipers were formed in Dublin in 1977). Their first number was too punky for a hard-rock crowd and the sound mix was appalling. Almost immediately there was a general air of discontent, with shouts of 'Get off!' and more imaginatively 'Fuck off you bunch of tossers!' And that was from the sound engineers! I'd never heard such antagonism towards a support band. Admittedly, a large number of rock fans don't normally bother watching the warm up groups and therefore never have to confront their deep-rooted dislike of support bands. But the New Bingley Hall was in the middle of nowhere and it didn't have a bar, so not only did the fans have to endure queues, rain and raw burgers, they couldn't even get a bloody pint! The Vipers didn't stand a chance and one disgruntled fan who had enterprisingly sneaked beer into the venue, decided things were so bad that he was willing to part company with said beer and lobbed one of his cans at the lead singer. And wallop – it hit him right on the temple. Such accuracy of projectile throwing in such a cramped environment had to be admired and the anonymous thrower was rewarded with the fourth loudest cheer of the evening. This completely knocked the lead singer off his stride and he buggered off stage. This received the third biggest cheer of the evening and eventually having played gamely on, the rest of the band followed suit – closely followed by the second biggest cheer of the evening. Soon after, the lights came back on and the Vipers never returned.

Having now removed the support band after only a couple of minutes, it meant we had to stand there for another two hours before Lizzy came on. By this stage none of us were in the mood for close quarter rocking, so we stood at the back to give us room for a bit of free-form headbanging. At 9.45pm the lights went down and the biggest cheer of the night went up. As a crowd we were weary and it took Lizzy a little while to get us warmed up, but it wasn't long before we'd built up a good head of headbanging steam and by the time they took their first bow, the trials and tribulations of earlier seemed long forgotten.

It was the early hours of the morning when we finally got home. And the strange thing was that we'd all been in really good spirits on the way back. The four of us had really enjoyed the gig and when we said our goodbyes we all commented on what a great evening it had been.

The Concert Going Experience – Phase 1

Step 1: Queue to get in.

Step 2: Queue 10 deep at the bar for overpriced warm gnat's piss. This means that by the time you've been served and bought your two pints (you would buy a pair of pints so you wouldn't have to queue again) the first bell rings, followed immediately by the second and then the third (which makes you wonder why they don't just have one bell that rings for longer). This means you have to neck your pints because you can't take them into the venue as the bouncers are worried that once in your seat you might start lobbing them in the air.

Step 3: Wait another hour and a half because the lead singer is demanding a roast dinner.

Step 4: Finally, when the band come on, you have to join arm in arm with other male rockers because all the rock-chicks have been invited back stage.

I loved it really. I just got more cynical the older I got.

Long live rock'n'roll.

1979: On The Road (Age 17)

It seems to be a rites of passage thing, that every teenager needs to go on a road trip that will ultimately end in disaster. Our particular misadventure would end up with Paul Kossoff playing loudly, while our car headed at speed towards a tree and a telegraph pole. And yet, it all started so well.

It was the late summer of 1979. I was still not legally old enough to drink but the many lures of alcohol were starting to have a significant impact on my drinking behaviour. For one thing my perception of drink was that it was cool. And as they say in marketing, perception is king. And of course, my rock heroes reputations lived and died by how many hotel rooms they trashed and how many bottles of Jack Daniels they consumed. It seemed the bigger the band, the bigger the excess and the greater the hell-raising street credibility the bands created. Whether it was self-destructive or anti-social, it didn't seem to matter. It came across, on the most part, as a lot of good natured fun and I was always up for a bit of good natured fun.

That summer, Vivien had gone off for a month to see her friend who lived in Ilfracombe and Huw and I were off to join the two of them for the last week of Vivien's vacation. For me, it was going to be great to see Viv again and for Huw, it was a *sure-thing*.

Road Trip

It was 4.00pm, 180 miles to Ilfracombe, we had a tent, rock tapes, a tank full of petrol, a cooler-box full of beer, it was blazing hot and we weren't wearing sunglasses. We were ready! I phoned Vivien to say we should be there by 8.00pm and we set off down the M5 in my mum's mustard coloured Datsun Cherry. It really was a glorious afternoon. We made good progress and passed Gloucester in no time. We had Rory Gallagher, *Live! In Europe* blasting out of the tape recorder and my heart was alive with the day.

"This is what life's all about," I shouted to Huw. Huw nodded, but because the music was on so loud he probably hadn't even heard me. Rory finished his set and Deep Purple were next up. We were now passing Bristol.

"I've got a real thirst on," I shouted to Huw, "we got any Coke?"

Huw turned down the volume "What?"

"I said I've got a real thirst on, have we brought any Coke?"

"There's no need to shout…I didn't bring any, did you?"

"No, it looks like we've just got a fridge full of beer," I replied.

We looked at each other and silence prevailed. In every sense - other than the fact I was at the wheel of a car going 70 mph down the M5 - this was a perfect moment for a beer. Sun, rock music, we were on the first day of our holiday and we were both on for a sure thing. But no, we couldn't. I couldn't, I couldn't turn up drunk. After all, I hadn't seen Vivien for three weeks and I'd never even met her friend. It would be madness. And from a driving perspective, illegal.

"Go on then, let's just have the one," I said, as if Huw had actually asked me the question. He didn't need to. We both knew that once the concept of having a beer had been subliminally raised, it was inevitable. It was hot, we were thirsty and we had vast reserves of self-delusion, so it was easy to justify our actions. "I'll be alright with just the one can," I said.

Three hours later I turned round to Huw, "Are you okay?"

"I've banged my shin – where are we?" Huw was dazed and confused.

"I think we're in a ditch." I tried reversing but the car wouldn't budge. It's amazing how your body can change from a happy, drunken stupor to a miserable, drunken stupor in the space of seconds.

All sense of self-control had dissolved after the first sip. The moment had been too exhilarating for self-restraint and rational thinking. The drink had made us feel like hell raising rock heads with no regard for rules and regulations.

There had been four pubs mentioned as reference markers in the directions that Vivien had given me. We visited all of them as if it had been compulsory. And we had also consumed the entire contents of the alcohol in our cooler-box. Then as we'd approached Coombe Martin (just outside Ilfracombe) on the A399, the winding roads had become dark and narrow. And the tape had got louder and louder and our singing rowdier and rowdier and my speed faster and faster and the bends sharper and sharper and Paul Kossoff came on and was blasting out 'The Band Plays On,' and then…everything came to a thundering crescendo, quickly followed by an eerie silence.

We were now surrounded by bramble.

By the time we'd got out of the car and on to the road, three cars had stopped. Now things were serious. I was 17, drunk and I'd just driven my car into a ditch. This wasn't fun anymore. The ditch was about two feet deep which explained why the car hadn't responded to my reversing request. We surveyed the scene. We had gone straight off the road and flown into the ditch between a tree and a telegraph pole. The car was well hidden and the bramble must have cushioned our stop. Neither of us had been wearing our safety belts and two feet to the left or right and certain tragedy would have resulted. One of the drivers offered to give us a lift to the nearest garage and on seeing we were okay, the other two drivers left the scene.

Eventually we were towed out of the ditch and we were able to continue our journey. Strange, but the driver of the tow truck, who was fully aware my senses were significantly impaired by drink, never questioned the fact I was getting back at the wheel of the car I had crashed not an hour earlier.

The time was approaching 11.00pm and it had been seven hours since we had set off and we were now three hours late. There were no mobile phones in those days and at no time during our journey had we stopped to phone Vivien to update her on our progress. As we pulled into the drive of her friend's parents' house, Vivien and her friend rushed out the door.

"Where have you been? We've been worried sick!" Vivien shouted at me as she ran to the car. What could I say? I presented a very sorry picture. I stank of alcohol, my eyes were bloodshot, my clothes were dirty from the brambles, the car was covered in mud and my voice was slurred. Excuses were futile. They had booked a table at a nearby restaurant and had planned a great night out for us. As soon as she saw me, she knew. We had been going out for over two years and in that time we had never had so much as an argument; sure I sulked a lot, but I was a teenager in love – that was allowed, but arguments…never. We hadn't seen each other for three weeks and I had really, really missed her. She looked at me, burst into tears and ran back to her friend for comfort. She didn't even give me a hug.

We were hell raising rock heads with no regard for rules and regulations. We were cool…real cool. I'm not ashamed to admit I cried that night. I despised myself for what I'd done: nearly killed myself, my best friend and devastated the girl I loved more than anything in the world. Had I hit the tree or the telegraph pole there would have been no pedestal for us, no eulogy to say we 'lived the dream', just heartbroken loved ones wondering how we could have been so stupid and what a waste of two young lives. Mundane my working life may have been, but I couldn't handle the destruction of being 'on the road.' That night I was glad I wasn't a rock star.

****

On the 8th November 1979, one day after my 18th birthday, we went to see AC/DC at the New Bingley Hall in Birmingham. This was the first time I had seen them with their new lead singer Brian Johnson. He had previously been a member of a band called Geordie. We queued, we avoided raw burgers, we kept hold of our tickets and the crowd behaved themselves and 'put up' with the support band, some outfit called Def Leppard. AC/DC were superb. The first album AC/DC released with Brian Johnson was *Back in Black,* and the rest, as they say, is history.

The previous night I'd had a big celebration down The Swan, with lots of friends coming along to wish me a happy 18th birthday. When Gordon (the landlord) enquired as to the nature of our celebration he looked a bit surprised, then he looked a bit perplexed and then he looked at me with an expression that told me he had known all along. Gordon was a great landlord.

Chapter 27

The Gig Scene
(1979 Continued. Age 18)

10 Years Later - 26th November 1979
(Birmingham Odeon, £3.00, Front Stalls, B17)

The Fastest Guitarist In The West

It had been a while since I'd been to a gig with just the lads, not that I was complaining as I loved going with Vivien; but I knew the next one on the horizon wouldn't be her cup of tea and it was one that all the lads 'needed' to attend – the mighty '10 Years After'. Well, '10 Years Later' to be exact, as it was 10 years since Alvin Lee had performed with his band at Woodstock.

When you think about it – from a musical perspective - an amazing amount had happened in the

10 years following the 1969 Woodstock festival. Hard rock, prog rock, heavy rock and punk rock had all grown, blossomed and were now (supposedly) wilting. As far as I was concerned though, there was still plenty of life left in rock music and the chance to see a legend like Alvin Lee required little or no mental effort.

Ten Years After were an English blues-rock band, and between 1968 and 1973 they achieved eight Top 40 albums on the UK Albums Chart.

I was a bit worried that it would be sold out, so I was absolutely chuffed to get tickets downstairs in the second row. This man deserved respect. This had the potential to be one of the best gigs of all time. Alvin Lee, I mean…it was Alvin 'friggin' Lee. We counted down the days.

The Gig

We got to the concert just in time for the support, the Bogey Band, but quickly wished we hadn't, as we were virtually the only ones there, which in a 2,500 seater venue was slightly eerie. We quickly headed to what we thought would be a packed bar. But once again, it was strangely quiet.

"The place will soon fill up with old rockers and hippies," I said to the lads to reassure them that we hadn't made an almighty faux-pas by buying tickets for a washed up dinosaur. "They're far too hip to arrive for the support band. They'll all still be down the pub…where we should have stayed." General nods of agreement ensued and we went and ordered another pint. The bells rang, but we didn't need to panic as we had seats in the front stalls.

"I bet the atmosphere's really building up in there," I said, as the atmosphere in the bar was non-existent. The lads feigned more general nods of excitement.

I needed to inject a bit of enthusiasm into them. "Right let's go!" I shouted and jumped up with a spring in my step. "Let's go and watch the legend." So we marched purposefully out of the bar and into…a virtually empty arena. This was my 46th concert and I'd never seen anything like it. The place looked like a scene from a *Zombie* movie, with a few brain-dead rockers wandering around aimlessly – so we pointed the band back towards the stage door, then the few hundred or so of us that were there waited for them to appear.

One rocker shouted out 'Wally,' but it got no response. Finally the lights went down, followed by a half-hearted cheer and then the sight of *excited* rockers strolling down to the front to join us. By now we had taken the few steps forward to stand by the stage.

Lee looked like a rock'n'roll casualty and seemed to rely on long meaningless solos. His performance at the Woodstock Festival had supposedly helped catapult him to stardom. Stardom must be a very fragile and transient place.

The few hundred of us at the front of the stage, clapped and cheered respectfully, but there was no spark. I could see the lads were struggling to get into the gig and the last thing we needed to hear was a long drawn out drum and bass solo.

"Put your hands together for Tom Compton on drums," said Lee. I didn't dare look at Huw, Paul or Steve. I just kept my eyes firmly fixed on the stage.

During Tom's drum solo I pondered on why the place was so empty. Was it that the hippies had all moved on and become part of mainstream society? Had the '70s rockers become punks or was it simply that Alvin Lee's brand of rock-blues was dead and had now been taken over by the much heavier and rawer rock sound of the likes of AC/DC. Or, the scariest thought of all, were the scaremongers right? Was rock dead? I pondered this and more until Compton and then Mick Hawksworth, the bassist, had finished amazing us with their improvised knowledge of…of what?…I could never quite work it out. But anyway we rewarded them with our most enthusiastic contrafribblarities.

Drum And Bass Solos

I remember seeing my first drum solo at the Rainbow gig on 11th September 1976. The band had been on for about 60 minutes and they were half way through another Rainbow classic, when Dio suddenly shouted "Cozy Powell" and pointed at the great skin man, to which we all gave loud shouts of "Yeeeeesssssss!" And clapped our hands above our heads. At that point all the other band members buggered off stage and the lights darkened, except for one big spotlight that was focused on Cozy's massive kit. We had just entered the 'drum solo zone.'

To see a drum solo for the first time is a truly awe-inspiring experience, especially when you're aged 14 and have been brought up on a diet of Top of the Pops, with drummers caressing their kits with a feather duster. Cozy was the real deal and I felt a sense of pride that he could kick ass on the drums. However, the drum solo was a bit like a drug, but without the addiction. In other words nothing ever lived up to the adrenaline-fuelled buzz of the first time. It was just a downhill slope, with each solo indistinguishable from the next, until it became one big beat infested haze. I mean, what were we supposed to do during these periods of self-indulgence, other than to stand there and look totally expressionless…while pondering if the bar was still open.

We continued to shout and salute Alvin, and at the end of the concert he thanked each and every one of us individually with a handshake.

The only positive thing to come out of this gig was that for the first time in my concert-going career I got an item of memorabilia that was thrown into the crowd - a drum stick. And I was left to ponder where I could stick it?

****

If there was a change of attitude then rock, in many ways, had contributed to its own fall from grace, by forgetting who the most important people were – the fans. The biggest bands had lost touch with reality. The wait for them to come on stage was getting longer, while the concerts were getting shorter and the ticket prices were getting higher. The stages were getting further and further away, while the solos were getting longer and longer and the band members were getting more and more self-indulgent. There is a thin dividing line between self-indulgence that is revered because it's perpetuating an image and self-indulgence that is, well....... self-indulgent and charmless. It just seemed to me that some of the bands were losing respect and empathy for their fans.

Review from the Birmingham Evening Mail

Nothing changes

Alvin Lee, Odeon, New Street, Birmingham

TEN years ago Alvin Lee was the lead guitarist with Ten Years After – one of the biggest names in rock music.

Now it's Ten Years Later, and as Lee says: "Nothing changes."

He is still the maestro of the late '60s rock, characterised by a strong blues influence, powerful riffs, lots of string-bending, thumping bass and long improvisations that wander into self-indulgence.

There is an excellent cameo from bassist Mike Hawksworth, and even a drum solo from Tom Compton.

Naturally enough these are only intervals in the Alvin Lee show.

Lee is at his best on extended blues like Sonny Boy Williamson's "Help Me" in which he bottlenecks to the manor born and plays a stunning harmonica.

TOM REID

Chapter 28

The Gig Scene
(1980 – Age 19)

The lads had been disappointed with the Alvin Lee gig and I felt with their A-levels approaching next June and University around the corner, they were moving on from the scene. But for me the scene had always been much more than just the music, it had been a way to express myself and I wasn't ready to let go of what had become an integral part of my identity. Besides, I had no other direction in which to go.

I continued to listen out for new bands and it wasn't long before I was back in Reddington's Rare Records delving into...well, whatever bands I could find. Like, Montrose, Head East, Point Blank, Teaze, Legs Diamond, Triumph, Yesterday & Today, Zon and April Wine, to name but a few.

One subgenre of rock that I didn't really get into, that was flourishing in the USA in the early 1980s, was glam-metal (also known as hair metal). To me it came down to one simple thing – I just didn't connect with the music.

New Wave Of British Heavy Metal

In 1978 AC/DC had breathed new life into rock music. The American and Canadian Import scene had then kept the genre on its feet, but now as we moved into the 80's, the tides of change were just too strong and rock was flat out on its back and new wave music was in, with bands like Depeche Mode, The Cure, Duran Duran and Talking Heads riding the waves of this burgeoning musical genre. And now I couldn't be in denial any longer. The hatchet merchant that was punk music had ruthlessly dismissed bands like Budgie, Wishbone Ash, Barclay James Harvest, Gillan, Steve Hillage, Alvin Lee, Camel, UFO, Yes and countless others. And now to make things worse, bands like Purple and Sabbath had also lost their mojo. This left a big gap in the market.

Fortunately waiting to fill the gap was the New Wave of British Heavy Metal (NWOBHM). Phew!

It had started in the late 1970s and was now ready to explode on to our turntables. And it wasn't long before it revitalised the rock scene.

In effect the NWOBHM represented the second wave of heavy metal music in the UK. And what was noticeable about this new brand of heavy rock was that the bands were less blues influenced and were basically stripping everything back down to basics.

For me, it all started with a gig on the 27th April 1980 at Wolverhampton Civic Hall, where I witnessed the fresh and exciting sound of Saxon. But the real launch day, the day when I knew something new, magical and significant was happening occurred 41 days later.

Iron Maiden had entered the building.

Iron Maiden - 7th June 1980

(Birmingham Odeon, £3.00, Centre Stalls, S44)

By now the pre-gig drink had become an integral part of the evening's entertainment. It had been a gradual progression. In the early years, gigs were alcohol-free affairs in which we took in every aspect of the evening. Then we moved on to sitting round a communal pint in the Odeon bar, still engaging in the holistic experience. Then we graduated to all having our own pint (still in the Odeon bar), but rarely missing any of the support acts. Eventually we moved on to meeting at pubs outside the venues (for half an hour or so) and that meant the support bands had competition in the form of 'Mickey Mouse' (lager and bitter) and Brew XI. Soon the support bands didn't stand a chance - our pre-gig meeting times got earlier and earlier and the number of pints being consumed was increasing at a steady rate.

The Gig

Iron Maiden would turn out to be one of the biggest bands to come out of the NWOBHM scene (if not the biggest), but at this stage in their career my knowledge of their repertoire was scant. But even so, I still managed to convince Vivien and Huw to join me to see if they were any good or not.

We met in The Duck on Hagley Road (on the outskirts of Birmingham) for a couple of quiet drinks that were then followed by a few noisier ones in the Odeon bar. Soon the final bell went and we entered the stalls to see Maiden on their first major tour. The atmosphere was electric and when the lights went down a number of rear and mid stall fans ran to the front.

I want to briefly return to the 'running-to-the-front' sub-culture, as it had its own set of rules and regulations that need to be explained. The timing of this fervent ritual was, in most cases, dependent on the 'heaviness' of the band. Progressive rock bands very rarely necessitated the need for a front of stage onslaught and typically people would remain in their seats until the encore, when they would stand up and clap along. Standard rock bands like Wishbone Ash, Budgie, Blue Oyster Cult or Bad Company would usually stimulate the crowd somewhere around the first encore and a run-to-the-front assault would often occur at this point. The real heavy, intense and loud rock bands like AC/DC, Motorhead, and Rainbow always required a run-to-the-front immediately upon the lights going down. That was the tradition, that's how it had always been and everyone knew it: the fans, the staff and the bands. And Maiden were most definitely lights out, heads down, run-to-the-front material.

So it was, as the rear stall boys started to run past our row S seats that we leapt out to join them. But this time it was different. The security guards, who stood between the front stalls and the cheaper seats, seemed bigger and nastier. I mean, fair enough they had gone through the motions of trying to stop crowd surges before, but it had always been a token gesture and had only delayed the inevitable charge by a few minutes. This new breed of security guard clearly meant business and after they easily resisted the first wave of attack, I got the feeling an immediate second wave would be futile. I was in shock. What was the world coming to? First they start checking every ticket individually, so you can't get down from the circle to the stalls and now you can't even run to the front. The good old days seemed to be drifting away.

My thoughts were interrupted by the familiar sound of drums, bass, guitar, more guitar and vocals.

Iron Maiden had arrived.

The first bars of the first song were as good an introduction to the world of big time touring as I had heard but, sitting in my seat, I felt like a caged tiger with a harem full of tigresses sitting outside the cage: excitement and frustration, all in one emotion. I was cursing those pesky security-guards for preventing me from enjoying myself.

Eventually everyone stood up, which was a great relief, as headbanging in your seat always has that air of rock-loser about it, whereas, of course, headbanging in the traditional standing, legs wide-apart, back arched stance is rock-winner territory. So now I was a lot happier and occasionally I would have a rest from headbanging to observe Huw and Viv in full flow. Vivien always managed to create a huge disturbance with her long red hair without actually adopting a conventional headbanging motion; it was more of a rock dance or freak-out as she liked to call it. Whatever it was, it looked the business.

Finally, as the band stormed into *Phantom of the Opera*, there was a renewed sortie towards the stage. We broke through the first and only line of defence without any resistance because (it appeared that) the security guards had been given the all-clear to let the mob through. I was in such a frenzy to get to the front that I completely lost Huw and Vivien, but I didn't mind as I was there in the mix, jumping up and down, arms in the air, head shaking and once again in the wonderful world of ROCK!

"Yes, yes, yes, wooooooooooooo, that was awesome," I said, as we exited the Odeon.

"Fab," added Vivien.

"My head hurts," grunted Huw.

"They were as tight as a camel's arse in a sandstorm," I said, tapping into my extensive knowledge of similes.

"So were their spandex pants," said Vivien, who was temporarily in a dream world that didn't involve me.

"No, my head really does hurt," Huw continued to grunt. I ignored both their comments.

"Technically, that was probably one of the best bands I've ever seen," I said with total ignorance of what constituted technical greatness.

"I'm not friggin' joking, I think you'd better call me an ambulance," Huw *really* grunted this time.

As it turned out Huw was just suffering from what is known as post traumatic headbanging disorder (or PTHD as it is usually referred to), of which the only known cure is a few pints of real ale, which we administered forthwith and hey presto, an hour later he was cured.

This tour was imaginatively called the 'Iron Maiden' tour, in support of their eponymous debut album and it was their first solo headlining tour (it followed their co-headlined 'Metal for Muthas' tour from earlier in the same year). And the gig was so good that I had to find a way of including it in my top five gigs of all-time list.

My Top Five *(six)* **Gigs of All Time**

1. AC/DC, 9th Nov 1978, Birmingham Odeon

2. Lynyrd Skynyrd, 2nd Feb 1977, Birmingham Odeon

3. Rainbow, 11th Sept 1976, Birmingham Odeon

4. Rush, 3rd June, 1977, Birmingham Odeon

5= Rory Gallagher, 21st April 1978, Birmingham Odeon

5= Iron Maiden, 7th June 1980, Birmingham Odeon

Review from the Birmingham Evening Mail

Maiden make it warm

Iron Maiden, Odeon, New Street

For a sixth-month-old band on their first major tour, Iron Maiden earned the roaring reception they won from Birmingham fans.

But the nuts and bolts of their stage act still need work. While the five-man band brought some welcome fresh ideas to a heavy metal performance, the tight sound that marked their first album was often missing on stage.

Technical hitches marred parts of their show.

But for the fans, the sheer excitement of the set more than made up for its faults.

Some of the slower tracks such as Remember Tomorrow showed Maiden at their best, with impressive lead guitar work from Dennis Stratton.

And by the time the band pounded into Phantom of the Opera several fans were storming the stage amid deafening calls for encores.

JACKIE BAILEY

****

The second coming of heavy rock meant that there were a whole new set of bands to get into - cue Reddington's Rare Records. I soon had in my collection, singles from Samson, Sledgehammer, Tygers of Pan Tang, Praying Mantis, Witchfynde, Trespass, Triarchy, Fist, Tank, Dark Star, Vardis, Dedringer and Borich, to name but a few.

Like the birth of British rock music 10 years or so earlier, the NWOBHM spawned three bands that were to reign supreme: Def Leppard, Iron Maiden and Saxon (although Saxon never reached the commercial heights that Leppard and Maiden achieved). In Def Leppard's case, in order to achieve the success they craved they quickly distanced themselves from the NWOBHM tag and opted for a sugary sweet, highly polished, Mutt Lange produced sound that found them a mainstream audience – predominately in the USA, where I believe their albums sold quite well. But ultimately this came at a cost to their metal fan-base in the UK.

The End Is Nigh

It was nearly time. Maybe I didn't know it back then, but it was…it was nearly time. Soon the lads and Vivien would be gone. They were starting University and leaving me to ponder life at the Birmingham Rates Office. It had been a while since all of us had been present for a gig so it was time for one last group excursion to the land of rock. We were going to the first ever Monsters of Rock Festival at Donnington.

The First Monsters of Rock Festival - 16th August 1980

(Donnington. Rainbow, Judas Priest, Scorpions, April Wine, Riot, Saxon, Touch. £7.50, Ticket No. 30628)

I hated festivals. I'd never been to one but I instinctively knew that I hated them. It was 16th August 1980, it was 5.00am and my alarm had just gone off. This was the first time in my life that I had got up before 10.00am on a Saturday and it was taking me a while to adjust to the time-zone difference.

We set off in two cars. Vivien, Huw, Steve and me in my mum's Datsun Cherry and our equivalent of the fifth Beatle: Craig, aka…Balls-eye, travelling with Paul and Balls-eye's girlfriend in his red Mini. Balls-eye had been a regular feature of our group in respect of the local scene but prior to this festival he had never joined us at a gig.

We arrived on the outskirts of Donnington Park at 7.00am and quickly settled into the one-inch-an-hour speed limit, before entering the ground at 10.00am. 10.00am! The first band wasn't due on until 1.00pm. What the flip were we meant to do for three hours in a muddy field?

We found a place to sit someway from the stage and started on the neat vodka. We had heard that you wouldn't be allowed to take in alcohol, so we disguised the vodka in a bottle of pop. I hate Vodka. Had I been under surveillance, it wouldn't have been difficult for security to have figured out that our pop bottle may not have contained what it said on the label, as I followed each swig with convulsions and pained grimaces.

"Well this is nice. Whose bloody stupid idea was this?" All eyes turned on me, which created a subliminal answer to Paul's question. I felt uncomfortable when the spotlight was on me, especially when I had no idea what I was going to say, so I took another swig of my breakfast and performed more convulsions. There was a momentary silence.

"Festivals are about the atmosphere, the kudos, and about the fact you can say you were there," said Huw, who had just had a sip of *pop* and was trying his best to hide the after effects.

"Yeah, it's about the mud, the rain, the lack of sleep and spotting the band when you hear some noise coming from yonder." Paul wasn't a happy man. Paul liked his home comforts and had come to the festival more out of a sense of group loyalty than desire. There was another brief silence.

"Don't look now, but you should see the state of those rockers arriving over there."

We all immediately looked round to see a bunch of hardened bikers. Balls-eye, whose comment had brought them to our attention was a conservative rocker and didn't like the ugly biker type metal-heads that we were all now gawking at. As they made their way through the crowd, you could tell everyone was praying they wouldn't make camp near their own. Fortunately they passed our pitch and eventually settled down in a space that, strangely enough, no one had noticed right near the front. They really were the rock heads from hell. The only way I can describe them is that they were like a bunch of Lemmy look-alikes. And the men didn't look much better either.

As we all breathed a sigh of relief, Vivien re-focused our minds…"I spy, with my little eye, something beginning with S." Oh yes, it was going to be a fun-packed three hours before the first band came on. We went through all the obvious answers like shoes, sky and shit, and the less obvious answers like safe-to-eat burgers, single blade of grass, and soap and the downright ridiculous answers like soul-boys, sense and sun. But after about half an hour we still hadn't got it and so we gave up. The answer was 'Stage.' When it's that difficult it's simply not worth playing.

At 1.00pm we could just about make out something was happening on the stage and we presumed it was the first band but by the time the sound waves had reached us they had finished their set.

The spaces around us started to fill up and following Touch, the next band on were Saxon. Just before they were due on I made a dash for the toilets. Finding the bogs was fine (and 'bog' was an apt description for the state of the toilets) but it took me ages to locate where we had made our pitch, by which time Saxon had come and gone.

"Were Saxon any good?" I asked when I returned.

"Who?" they all said in unison.

This wasn't turning out how I'd imagined it. Riot were on next.

"Riot are the bollocks," I said during the 30 minute break. "They're one of the top new rock bands from America. *Warrior* from their album Rock City is an absolute anthem. So are we all up for a bit of headbanging when they come on? The whole atmosphere needs a kick up the arse and we need to start to get into this festival."

"You can," said an unenthusiastic Steve.

"Yeah, we'll follow your lead," said Huw sarcastically.

Balls-eye simply shook his head. He didn't like headbanging.

The MC for the day was Neal Kay - a London-based DJ who, along with Tommy Vance, was a significant factor in the rise of the New Wave of British Heavy Metal. "Donnington, put your hands together for RIOT!" The place exploded into a whimper. Riot were definitely on stage and they appeared to be playing their instruments but the combination of broad daylight and a terrible sound quality took away from their performance and even though I did stand up for *Warrior*, it was a short-lived affair, as not one other person in the crowd joined me and as a consequence I felt a touch self-conscious and so sat back down. More vodka nurse!

It is alleged the Rainbow sound engineers hogged all the time on the sound mix so when the support bands came on, it was a total shambles and their performances were spoilt.

After Riot I needed a nap, as I was tired following my *breakfast*. After about 15 minutes I was woken by Vivien to find Castle Donnington had suddenly sprouted an amazing roof, full of moving objects. Wow, that Vodka was strong!

"My mouth feels like the bottom of a…" Before I'd had time to finish the sentence, a plastic bottle narrowly missed my throbbing head.

"Quick, take cover!" said Huw.

I looked around to see a distinct absence of cover. We were in the middle of a bloody field.

"Excuse my ignorance but where exactly am I meant to take …?" There's nothing like a swift, sharp blow to the back of your head to bring you to your senses. I quickly joined the others and we used our coats and the cardboard we had been sitting on to create a shield wall that King Harold II would have been proud of. Under our shield, we debated the goings on outside of our den.

"Never seen this happen at the Odeon," said Steve stating the bleeding obvious.

'No, it appears they are lobbing their holy bottles of piss in any direction without counting to three." I love a *Holy Grail* reference and Huw's comment lifted our spirits.

"Give me the palatial, dry and warm Birmingham Odeon any day," Paul said, quickly downing our spirits.

"I have never seen so many bottles, cans and plastic receptacles flying simultaneously through the air in all my life." I said in a state of bewilderment.

"There are so many that for a moment I thought Donnington had a god-damn roof."

"It touches my heart," Steve said, "35,000 of us packed into Donnington race course and when you feel thirsty or run out of beer, a friendly rocker is more than happy to lob a bottle or can in your direction."

"Yeah, but mine tastes a bit strange," said Paul. General laughter could be heard from under our temporary and dry safe haven.

"Don't worry lads, they'll soon get bored and stop," said Balls-eye, ever the pragmatist. And when, as Balls-eye predicted, the crowd did indeed get bored of the throwing-the-piss-bottle game, we re-surfaced to see April Wine.

The only time the bottle lobbing behaviour returned was later in the evening and this time it was aimed at a plane that was flying overhead and drowning out the sound from the stage. I don't think the pilot realised how much he was pissing off *us* rockers, but I'm damn sure he got the message when he saw all those bottles and cans flying upwards and missing his plane by the narrowest of half-mile margins. You've got to give it to some rockers, they do try their damnedest to perpetuate that loser tag.

April Wine were not as good as when I'd seen them at the Odeon on 7th March. Scorpions were crap and Judas Priest looked pissed.

When Priest finished their set, we could finally see the light at the end of the tunnel. Yes, we were there for the festival as a whole, but the big draw was Rainbow and this was Cozy Powell's last gig with the band. For some inexplicable reason Cozy must have thought he had a proper job and was polite enough to give notice of his intention to leave. I had always been under the impression that when a band member left it was because he had died, or he'd been fired, or he'd disappeared mid tour. But to give notice? *Naagghhh*. Take Jeremy Spencer, the ex-guitarist with Fleetwood Mac - he allegedly disappeared in the middle of their US tour and joined a religious cult. You almost feel a kind of respect for him in a 'well-done for reinforcing the rock myth' kind of way, because, of course, normal behaviour simply isn't acceptable for our rock-gods.

We learnt post festival that because Graham Bonnet - Rainbow's lead singer – had had the temerity to have his hair cut short it cost him the coveted lead singer position in Rainbow. So Donnington turned out to be his last gig…only unlike Cozy, he was fired on the spot and booted out! Now that's more like it.

So Rainbow were about to come on…well we thought they were about to come on, but it turned out we had another two hours to wait. Anyway, Huw decides he needs to go to the toilet, which in itself is fine as long as you can find your way back. Forty five minutes later and Huw had not found his way back. Problem. I weighed up the options.

1.   Shout out 'HUW', at the top of my voice. Futile as people might think Huw is a lost roadie and before I'd had time to gauge a reply, the whole crowd would be shouting for Huw

2.   Ask the person next to me if he's seen my mate Huw. I was annoyed that this one had even entered my head.

3.   Phone him. A brilliant idea, but I quickly had to shelve it as mobile phones had not yet been invented.

4.   Drink more vodka and hope for a miracle. Best idea so far.

5.   Randomly walk around and hope that I find him among the 35,000 people.

Option five seemed the most sensible, so I told Viv to waive her coat in the air so I wouldn't lose a fix on our position and I started walking randomly around.

Seconds passed. Minutes passed. I was starting to think option 5 wasn't such a good idea after all. And Viv's coat waiving activities were sporadic to say the least and I was worried that I too would become detached from the group. Then all of a sudden I heard a voice…

"Pete!" I looked around. A sea of rockers, but no Huw.

"PETE!" This time it was louder and accompanied by the instantly recognisable smile of my best mate Huw. We gave each other a big hug and then we quickly looked from side to side to see if any of the crowd had noticed. They hadn't, so we gave each other another hug and then accused each other of being gay. In ricocheted response we both turned round to face the stage and simultaneously adopted the archetypal macho air guitar position. This may have looked a tad strange as the band hadn't actually come on yet.

Eventually we made our way back to the others, and by this time the coat waving duty had been passed over to Craig as he was the tallest, which made me wonder why I hadn't thought of that in the first place.

"Rainbow, Rainbow, Rainbow," we chanted, more in the hope that they would bloody hurry up than in adulation. We had all been up a long time and we were tired, bruised, battered, covered in mud and despite the seemingly endless supply of liquid filled bottles, dehydrated.

Eventually, the stage lights went down and for a second the whole of Donnington seemed to be in darkness and then bang, the *rainbow* lit up, the band ran on stage and 35,000 fans forgot how miserable they were.

Rainbow were brilliant. They had kept us waiting for well over an hour but, to be fair, the gig needed to be seen out of daylight. It was also boosted by (finally) a decent sound system and by the fact we all stood up.

Rainbow finished at 11.15pm and we were all really buzzing from the energy of their set. Well, almost all of us. Paul was more wheezing than buzzing. As we made our way back to our cars, there was mixed emotions about the day as a whole.

"I know this is the first Monsters of Rock festival, but I can't see it being mentioned in the same breath as Woodstock or the Isle of Wight." Paul had a point.

"Yeah, but it's one we will remember all our lives," said Steve. He was right, but the memories would not solely be about the music.

I added my thoughts, "It was good, very good and a great experience. And come on, we've had a laugh - haven't we?"

"Yeah, but Paul's got a point. It wasn't a classic," said Huw.

"But Rainbow were ace…fab, and we did have a good freak out at the end." Vivien was also right and at the end of the day, if you leave on a high, then the pain of the hours preceding it can quickly be forgotten.

"Shall we concentrate on finding our cars?" Balls-eye had spoken and we duly obeyed, finally getting home at 2.00am. At times it had felt more like a test of endurance than a rock gig, but nevertheless it was an experience that I was to repeat the following year. I don't know why, I hate bloody festivals.

As Paul had predicted the festival was not to go down as an important benchmark in rock festival history. It was panned by the critics.

That said, it has the kudos of being the first ever Monsters of Rock festival and the "I was there" bragging rights for all those who attended. And of course, there is much more to the festival experience than just the music.

Vivien freaking-out at Monsters of Rock festival, 16th Aug 1980

Chapter 29

Growing Up
(Dec. 1980. Age 19)

In September 1980 the lads and Vivien moved away to start university.

The subsequent Christmas they were back and we had arranged to meet up for a reunion. We were on a pub crawl. Paul, Huw and Steve were present and we were meeting Vivien later.

We chatted until we were up to date with each other's lives and then Huw steered the conversation around to his changing tastes in music. "I remember, years ago, listening to *The Boys Are Back in Town,*" Huw said, "and thinking, yes, things are good, we are the boys. But university life has changed all that...flares are definitely out. I Remember the first night I went to the uni bar, I had my patchwork quilt jeans on...you know, the one's with the Coca Cola cocaine patch on the back..."

We nodded.

"Well, I went from feeling cool to feeling like a novelty in an instant. Then one of the lads I got to know played me *All Mod Cons* by The Jam and I listened to it and thought, shit, lyrics with a meaning! What the fuck have I been listening to for the past six years?"

I thought carefully about what Huw had said. "But rock music is maligned and ridiculed by others because they don't get it, because its meaning is much

267

more existential than other forms of music and when people don't understand things, they instantly try to undermine it. Punk music was much more overt and was easier to define and understand; people feel more comfortable with that, even if they don't agree with its message or like its image. People hate not knowing. They hate to think there's some secret meaning to something – so they try and ridicule it. That's why we were marginalised. Because most people just didn't understand what rock music was about. In the end by being marginalised it surely gave us credibility not novelty value?"

There was a pause while we supped our ale.

"But things have changed," Huw said. "The credibility of rock has been devalued, you know that Pete, it was lost in a sea of self-indulgence. And so change was inevitable. The new wave…the energy is as much in the lyrics as it is in the music. Don't you think rock lacks that – that it's become too detached?" Huw asked.

"Absolutely not, I think rock always had a message, but it wasn't necessarily always in the lyrics. As I've said, it was much more subtle than that." I paused for no other reason than to punctuate the moment. "Look, it's simple, we were four boys on the edge of discovering life and we were going to do it together. Rock and youth, they make you feel like anything is possible. Punk music might have been around the edges of our world, but in the end it just created an extra layer of interest and never stripped away the core foundations of what we liked. You know: guitars, fast solos, bombastic lead singers, loud drums and the ringing in our ears the day after a concert. Rock music connected with us because it was in our DNA. We never had a choice. We were born to rock."

We all clinked our glasses together and took another sup from our quickly diminishing pints. At that moment Vivien entered the pub which created a natural ending point to our debate and for the next couple of hours, it was like nothing had changed and I was as happy as a man could be. But my happiness was short lived as that night I thought long and hard about what Huw had said. Maybe he was right, rock *was* dead, not just musically, but in terms of everything it represented. And all I was doing was sticking up for something that was no longer relevant. Maybe I was becoming the embodiment of the rock dinosaur we had so reviled – unable to move on and embrace a new world. Yes, AC/DC had lifted rock off the canvas and the NWOBHM had given some much needed CPR to the scene, but unfortunately the resuscitation had been short lived and the renewed optimism I had felt following the Iron Maiden gig had now evaporated. Huw had talked about The Jam like they were new and exciting, writing lyrics with meaning. Maybe I had become anachronistic, a misoneist, a total rock loser, floating adrift in an unrecognisable world. I felt worse than a professional masturbator who had just lost his 'World's Biggest Wanker' title.

Chapter 30

The Concert Going Experience – Phase 2

The pub gig: You start off virtually nose to nose with the lead singer as the band occupy a small floor space in a dive of a local pub. If the gig goes well they may be asked back again and they may start to play at other pubs in the local area.

Then if they're any good and they start to attract a loyal local following they graduate to pubs or clubs with a small stage about a foot high. As a fan you can still be right up there with the band but unless you're seven feet tall or the singer is vertically challenged you're no longer on their eye-line.

As their popularity grows, they move onto local concert venues with dedicated stages that are about waist high and are big enough for the band to walk around on. Now your eye-line is level with their knee-caps so if you stand at the front you have to permanently strain your head backwards to see the band. And actually getting to the front is now becoming a lot more difficult. You either have to arrive early and be first in the queue – which would mean sacrificing the pre-gig drink - or you have to let off a particularly evil fart that causes the crowd to scatter.

Then the A&R men start sniffing around and before you know it the band have signed a recording contract and they're moving on to the thousand-seater venues in which the stage is now guarded by bouncers and the floor is populated by annoying things called seats. Now you're lucky if you can make out the facial expressions of the band and you have to sit down because the bouncers have now decided they don't like anyone running to the front, standing up or basically enjoying themselves.

Finally the band really strikes it rich with their first album and they move onto the huge stadium circuit. Now the stages are over head high and so vast that they can accommodate a small symphony orchestra for that period in time when the band totally loses sense of reality. As a fan you're so far back that you're lucky if you can see the damn stage let alone the band. Now all you have left is the ultimate humiliation of spending time telling those unfortunate enough to stand next to you, how you once used to stand nose to nose with the lead singer.

Chapter 31

Growing Up
(1986 – Age 24)

In 1986, after nine years, my relationship with my first ever girlfriend – my rock-chick - came to an end. Vivien and I went our separate ways. I had loved Vivien with heart aching intensity, but the rock had gradually eroded from the chick and after she graduated in 1983 the free-spirit of the girl I first kissed at the Stourbridge disco in 1977 had been replaced with responsibility and ambition. Nothing wrong with that, but in truth, the later years of our relationship were held together by the earlier years and although we always got on really well, the kindred bond between us had gone. I was still in love, but with a person that no longer existed and it took me a long time to understand that. Vivien had simply chosen a more mature path on life's journey, whereas in my heart I was still a free spirited rock-head.

I felt so alone. So lost. And the pain…it ate away at me.

I was totally oblivious to the fact that the silver lining to my dark, dark clouds would one day make it all seem like it happened for the right reasons. But my wife Josephine was 7 years away and comforting words alluding to the fact that there were 'plenty more fish in the sea' was, at that moment in time, not what I wanted to hear.

****

I'm going to include some more lyrics by the same well-known country singer who's lyrics I included earlier, because again - at this juncture in the story – they fit perfectly.

Admittedly I'm not big on religion but hey, Mr Brooks makes the point well. The circle of life. But just to balance things up I've also added my own areligious interpretation of the lyrics. Hopefully, this won't cause offense, but there again I figure that no country fan will read this book so … rockers, atheists, devil worshippers … keep this bit to yourselves 😊

Just the other night at a hometown football game
My wife and I ran into my old high school flame
And as I introduced them the past came back to me
And I couldn't help but think of the way things used to be

She was the one that I'd wanted for all times
And each night I'd spend prayin' that God would make her mine
And if he'd only grant me this wish I wished back then
I'd never ask for anything again

Sometimes I thank God for unanswered prayers

She wasn't quite the angel that I remembered in my dreams
And I could tell that time had changed me
In her eyes too it seemed
We tried to talk about the old days
There wasn't much we could recall
I guess the Lord knows what he's doin' after all

And as she walked away and I looked at my wife
And then and there I thanked the good Lord
For the gifts in my life

Sometimes I thank God for unanswered prayers

© Garth Brooks "Unanswered Prayers" (Lyrics shortened)

Just the other night at a hometown football game
My wife and I ran into my old high school flame
And as I introduced them the past came back to me
And I couldn't help but think of the way things used to be

She was the one that I'd wanted for all times
And each night I'd spend hoping beyond hope that she would be mine
And if it did happen, if it really did happen for all time
I'd never ask for anything again

Sometimes I thank my lucky stars for dashed hopes

She wasn't quite the angel that I remembered in my dreams
And I could tell that time had changed me
In her eyes too it seemed
We tried to talk about the old days
There wasn't much we could recall
I guess life works things out after all

And as she walked away and I looked at my wife
And then and there I thanked whoever was listening
For the gifts in my life

Sometimes I thank my lucky stars for dashed hopes

© Garth Brooks "Unanswered Prayers" (alternative lyrics by Pete Turvey)

Chapter 32

Learning to Play the Guitar: Part 8
(The Night Before My First Live Gig, October 2001. Age 39)

I was sitting in the dressing room waiting to go out to Wembley Stadium. Five nights. All sold out. I'd made it. I was famous. Rich beyond my wildest imagination. I looked at the table at the back of the room. I'd been very specific about my rider (*)…a bottle of Jack Daniels. I picked it up and drank it neat from the bottle. I looked around. The room was full of people. Men, women. Just looking at me. I recognised the men, but I didn't know any of the women. My head felt fuzzy. Ten minutes I heard somebody shout out. I sat down. I couldn't go on, not in ten minutes. The crowd would have to wait. I looked across at my guitar. It felt like the only friend I had, the only thing I could trust. I cast my mind back to how it used to be. Before I became famous. I didn't have much but I had all that I needed…a wonderful girlfriend and friends that I could trust. A thought came into my head, something somebody had said to me, I can't remember who it was, but he said, the less you own of material things the more you own of yourself. I didn't really know what he meant back then, but now I understood. I put my head in my hands. I felt so alone. And then, I started to cry…

…that's when I woke up, tears flooding down my face. The dream had seemed so real. It sent a shiver down my spine. It reminded me of how I'd felt the night I crashed my car while travelling down to Ilfracombe with Huw…that I was glad I wasn't a rock star. And then I looked across at my wife asleep in bed and I felt a warmth in my heart. Tomorrow, I will enjoy myself, nothing more, and then I'll pack my dreams away.

* A rider is a set of requests or demands that a performer sets as criteria for performance, which are usually fulfilled by the hosting venue. The rider typically covers things like food and drink…especially drink!

Chapter 33

Learning to Play the Guitar: Part 9
(Jackson Tor Hotel, Matlock - Post First Gig)

I was standing in the hotel toilet, looking at myself in the mirror; reflecting on the time when I first discovered rock music. Feelings of heart-warming nostalgia flooded through my body. It was the start of an uncharted journey that was fun, romantic, innocent and free from responsibility. The epicentre of our musical odyssey may have only centred around the years 1975 to 1981 but it afforded us a wonderful time of discovery and I feel very lucky to have lived through that period and been able to see virtually all of the great rock bands of that time, in relatively small venues with a great bunch of lads and with a great girl.

Life seemed so uncomplicated and simple back then. But nothing ever remains the same and life went on and as I had feared, the popularity of hard rock, heavy rock and prog rock dwindled significantly in the 1980s and pretty much disappeared altogether in the 1990s (the only exception being Guns N' Roses).

But of course the music had just gone into a period of hibernation, it had never died. Nor will it ever die…rock music will live on forever. Especially the music from the 1970's.

The gig in Matlock gave me the chance to re-live my youthful ambitions. It was a real high and at that moment, in my own mind, I was a rock-god. Ever since the summer of 1981, when I'd bought my first guitar, I'd wanted to taste what it was like to play those classic riffs and stand in front of an audience and be an axe hero. Finally, 20 years later, I achieved that ambition. It was an emotional moment and to have my mates there, Paul, Huw and Steve, who'd been on the rock journey with me from the start, was a perfect end to the dream.

That night, for a moment, I almost thought I was good. When I came off stage I was buzzing and full of happy adrenaline…and I'd only done two numbers in front of a small crowd of family and friends. But hey, what are friends and family for, if not to falsely build up your self-belief and confidence and help you into those fantastic Emperor's new spandex trousers.

But in truth, it was poor.

Had I reproduced that performance in front of a hardened bunch of rock-heads, then I'm sure my plectrum and my guitar - if it were anatomically possible - would have been inserted into a place where the sun don't shine.

The harsh reality is that I have neither the natural talent nor the dedication (nor the constitution for that matter) to reach the dizzy heights of guitar playing greatness. And in any case, I'd finally realised that my dream of being a rock star was not even a dream anymore, it had just been a teenage fuelled fantasy.

After the main band had finished for the evening, the DJ came on and the celebrations continued until the early hours. At one point we all gathered round for a token headbang to *All Right Now; Down Down* and

Smoke on the Water. Funny, when it had all finished and I was helping the DJ take his stuff to the car, I noticed a box with broken glass and a crumpled sign that said *break glass only if rock-heads enter disco*. Thoughts of our road trip to Barmouth came flooding back into my mind and I laughed to myself as I helped him on his way.

When everyone had gone, Huw, Paul, Steve and myself made our way to the hotel bar to have one last bottle of wine. (Of course…it didn't end up being just the one bottle :)

"Who'd have thought, over a quarter of a century ago, we'd all be sitting here drinking Chateau le Shlasseler," Paul got us off to a flying *Python* start *(The Four Yorkshiremen* sketch*)*.

"Aye, aye," we all said.

"Them days were really something special," I said in my worst Yorkshire accent.

"Aye, happy days, happy days," said Steve.

"You know, we didn't have much in the way of money," Huw began.

"Or fashion sense," added Paul.

"Or sense," continued Huw "but we sure had a good time."

"Do you remember the first concert we ever went to as a group?" As I posed this question I knew that for the next hour or so we would drift into an alcohol fused trip down memory lane that would involve large doses of fact, myth, exaggeration, rationalisation, satire, self-deprecation, euphoric recall and good old-fashioned delusion. We had set off on the classic rock journey with no idea of where we were going. At times we had looked like nerds, but we felt like the coolest cats in town.

And as the wine flowed we relived those magnificent concerts when we'd initiated the run to the front or started the *Wally* cries.

And we drank a toast to our departed rock gods.

More than anything we kept saying what a great time it had been for classic rock and heavy metal music.

We were drunk, happy and very mellow and at that moment we all sat back in our chairs and retreated into our own thoughts. Eventually we lifted our glasses and made a toast to 'the good old days.' As we went to sit back down I said "Aye. And you try telling the young people of today that, and they won't believe a word."

The End…..

….but not the end…

…rock'n'roll will live on forever. Beyond the hatred, beyond the wars, beyond the madness, and beyond the beyond.

Long Live Rock'n'Roll

For Those About To Rock
......We Salute You

My Top Five Rock Songs of All Time

1. *Lynyrd Skynyrd — Free Bird*
2. *UFO – Rock Bottom*
3. *Rory Gallagher – Shadow Play*
4. *AC/DC – Let There be Rock*
5. *Black Sabbath – Black Sabbath*

My Top Five Albums of All Time

1. *Led Zeppelin – Led Zeppelin*
2. *Black Sabbath – Black Sabbath*
3. *AC/DC – Highway to Hell*
4. *Rainbow – Rainbow Rising*
5. *Pink Floyd – Wish You Were Here*

Of course, there is no definitive top five list. It's all about personal taste and the context of a song in terms of your life.

Noticeably with the list above all the tracks are from the 1970's (apart from Zeppelin…1969). And they are the 5 tracks/albums I have listened to the most since they were released. And what's more…I never get tired of hearing them.

What Are They Doing Today?

Lads Annual Reunion 2017 *(Age 55)* **From left to right:**
Craig (aka Balls-eye); Huw; Paul; Pete; Steve

Lads Annual Reunion 2020 *(Age 58)* **From left to right:**
Huw, Steve, Pete, Paul, Craig

Lads Annual Reunion 2023 *(Age 61)* **From left to right:**
Pete, Steve, Huw, Craig, Paul

Huw:

Huw lives north of Leicester and still loves the vinyl scene, so much so, that he currently has 5 vintage HiFi systems in his house, listening mainly to 70s and early 80s rock. His other interests include wheeling and dealing in antiques and horticulture of a specialist kind.

Steve:

Steve is now based in the West Country, and continues to pray at the altar of rock, as well as indulging in his new passions…God, golf and conspiracy theories.

Paul:

Paul has four daughters and a pretty decent rock voice. He now lives in Brighton and still enjoys going to see the classic bands of the 70's.

Vivien:

Vivien emigrated to Australia so that she could marry a Scouser. She works as an optometrist and has two daughters. She still has fond memories of her time with that weird rock-head called Pete.

Craig:

Balls-eye is a multi-millionaire, and is based here, there and everywhere. He denies all knowledge of being a rock-head.

Pete:

I got married in 1997 to Josephine. I run a music memorabilia business called Freebird Memorabilia. We have a dog called Floyd. I still listen to classic rock but don't headbang anymore due to the fact it hurts my head. I still play the guitar (badly); paint (even worse); and I have recently written a novel called *The Poppy Killer* (a psychological thriller); and a book of short stories called *Life Is Like… A Book Of Short Stories (You Never Know What You Will Get Next)*, which is an eclectic mix of drama, comedy, and fantasy (all with one thing in common). My greatest wisdom is that life should always have a purpose but the destination (of that purpose) should always be subservient to the journey. Oh, and I still talk bollocks. Keep on rocking, rockers.

Appendix

Reviews from the Birmingham Evening Mail

EVENING MAIL. MONDAY, FEBRUARY 9, 1976

REVIEWS

Be - Bop on the right road

Be-Bop Deluxe,
Birmingham Town Hall.

THE flaming guitar, held triumphantly aloft by Bill Nelson like some kind of sacrifice to the audience was really unnecessary.

Be-Bop Deluxe had already proved themselves.

Be Bop have been heralded as one of the bands most likely to succeed this year. After watching them on Saturday night I'm convinced they will be.

The flashy guitar stunt, slightly dimmed what had been an evening of enlightenment.

The band's new album, "Sunburst Finish," contains some fine material, but it is a rather cold piece of work.

Be-Bop Deluxe, live, though, are totally different. On stage they are vibrant, especially lead guitarist, Bill Nelson, the band's songwriter.

The precision and excellence of Nelson is matched by the other members—Simon Fox on drum, bass player Charlie Tumahai, and keys man Andy Clarke.

They work as a very solid tight unit, though the star of the band is undoubtedly Nelson, and he obviously enjoyed the spotlight's glare.

His songs smack a little of Roxy Music at times, but the group's talent is there to see.

Doctors of Madness, the support band, are rather strange.

Their music is very aggressive and occasionally frightening.

But they also possess a high degree of musicianship which allied the theatrics of their act, could put them on the same road to success as Be-Bop De Luxe.

— KEN LAWRENCE

Be Bop Deluxe - 7th Feb 1976

Rick earns the raptures

Rick Wakeman,
Odeon, New Street,
Birmingham.

NEARLY 5,000 fans can't be wrong — and that's how many saw Rick and the English Rock Ensemble last night.

Rick dominated the centre stage, his long, blond hair flowing over a floor-length cape, and whirling like a dervish between innumerable keyboards.

The ensemble helped him do justice to his grandiose, finely - crafted musical pieces, whether about King Arthur's court, the wives of Henry VIII or journeys to the centre of the earth.

Musically, there was a fascinating array of textures from keyboards, even though they seemed a little loud.

Ashley Holt's vocals were strong and forceful, John Dunsterville played intelligent guitar and there were a soaring, joyous brass section and a lot of varied percussion.

It could have been rather pompous and over-serious, but the band clowned around a lot, and good humour was the order of the night.

DAVID CRITTEN

Rick Wakeman - 2nd May 1976

REVIEW

Clapton sets

great pace

by SANDY COUTTS

Eric Clapton Band, Odeon, New Street, Birmingham.

MIDLAND fans of Eric Clapton really got value for their money last night.

In addition to all their dreams coming true by seeing the guitar hero on stage, there was the added bonus of a brief appearance by Van Morrison.

The first number, a track from Clapton's new album, "No Reason To Cry," set the scene for a stunning set by an immensely together band.

Sergio Rodriguez on percussion and Yvonne Elliman and Marcy Levy providing back-up vocals give Clapton's latest band a really punchy sound, and guitarist George Terry is outstanding.

After a second slower number from the new record, Clapton gave the fans what they really wanted — one of his classics. This was "Layla," the first few notes from Clapton building up the expectation.

The band didn't let anyone down, although it was interesting to see that George Terry was the man behind the best guitar sounds on stage.

Then, surprise, surprise, on came Van Morrison to rapturous applause. A slow blues, a rocking version of "Rock Me, Baby" and he left. We could have listened to him all night.

But the band didn't allow the pace to slow down. "Tell The Truth" followed with Clapton and Terry battling it out for the title of the best axe man on stage.

After a fine version of the Blind Faith number "Can't Find My Way," by Yvonne Elliman there was, I felt, rather a poor version of "Knocking on Heaven's Door."

The set ended with a slow blues, really the only number in which Clapton did his guitar thing.

Perhaps it's because we have heard so many people play his solos before, but I felt they lacked punch and again I have to say that Terry's guitar playing sounded fresher and more electrifying.

But Clapton can still exchange riffs with anyone, and he has one of the best bands in the land at present.

Eric Clapton - 5th August 1976

292

C'mon feel the noise!

Rainbow,
Birmingham Odeon.

THIS was music for a generation happy to flirt with the risk of temporary brain damage.

Rainbow play heavy, thumping monotonous music excruciatingly loud. Perforated eardrums were always a looming danger

Overall, they are musically limited, though Richie Blackmore is a fast, dexterous guitarist

The presentation was spectacular, with a backdrop depicting a Gothic castle, and a huge arch electronically lit in the colours of the rainbow (in the wrong order).

Cozy Powell's drum solo, accompanying a recording of the 1812 Overture, injected wit and a blinding explosion into proceedings.

But it wasn't really my cup of decibels, and I got bored.

But Rainbow got a rapturous reception from a young, mostly male, packed house and you can't argue with that.

DAVID CRITTEN

Rainbow - 11th Sept 1976

Too much noise

Hawkwind,
Odeon, Birmingham.

TAKE AWAY Hawkwind's pain - producing amplification, the strobes, the pretty lights, the man with the gas mask, the Rudolph Valentino singer and some hammy theatricals and there's not a lot left.

They're a band who seem to have got trapped in a strange psychedelic time warp but they seem to have a lot of fans.

I'm not one of them and felt their immense noise did nothing more than stop me enjoying the lights.

On the other hand the support band, Tiger, know all about enjoyment. With Big Jim Sullivan on guitar, they have the enthusiasm and good musical ideas to market.

They had a hard job cutting through the anticipation but managed it confidently.

With numbers like "Blue Space" which took Sullivan's stunning guitar work and combined it with some gentle digs at today's pop, their forthcoming LP should be a winner.

SANDY COUTTS

Hawkwind - 16th Sept 1976

294

The new Rock superstars

Odeon, New Street, Birmingham.

THIN · LIZZY seem destined to be Britain's latest Rock superstars.

Not only were they acclaimed as such by last night's ecstatic audience, they also look the part.

Most important they play superb, gutsy, aggressive music with verve and style.

The last British rock band to have such a devastating effect on audiences were Status Quo, who until now have been unrivalled in the field of out-and-out rock.

But Thin Lizzy may knock even Status Quo from their perch.

Last night they delivered an electrifying, pounding performance which few bands could live with.

Such songs as "Rosaline" and "The Warrior" have helped raise Thin Lizzy from the also-rans to the front-runners.

Phil Lynott is an excellent singer/bassist, but it is the power and aggression of twin lead guitarists Brian Robertson and Scott Graham which makes Thin Lizzy one of the tightest, most entertaining and enjoyable bands in Britain.

KEN LAWRENCE

Thin Lizzy - 26th Oct 1976

Skyn head mania

Lynyrd Skynyrd,
The Odeon, Birmingham.

AMERICAN rock band, Lynyrd Skynyrd, received a 90-minute standing ovation in Birmingham last night.

From the moment they appeared on stage at The Odeon, hordes of fans leapt up to dance at the front, a sea of waving arms lashed into a frenzy by every note.

And Skynyrd deserved it. They are the American equivalent of The Rolling Stones for stage excitement, their Deep South sound coming from somewhere below the gut.

There's no fancy Jagger tricks, just three (later four) lead guitarists and a keyboard player conjuring up a hypnotic assault on the senses backed by a solid drummer and bass.

Only at the end, when they went over the top in their traditional encore tribute to Duane Allman, did the wall of sound block out the music.

Less exciting for the Skyn heads, was the supporting Californian group, Clover.

But they had more than three leaves to their rock score and, superbly lead by pedal guitarist John McFee, produced a tight mixed bag varying from blues to country pickin' — and even yodelling.

BRIAN GLOVER

Lynyrd Skynyrd - 2nd Feb 1977

Power still full on

Ian Gillan Band,
Odeon, Birmingham

AFTER two years of silence, the voice that once belted out the lyrics for Deep Purple has lost none of its power.

Gillan proved what his supporters have always known — he ranks among the greatest of rock screamers.

But last night's show was not all about one man, and the band played a set that had something for everyone.

For long periods Ray Fenwick dominated the stage, filling the air with some inspired extended riffs, and John Gustafson contributed a vocal performance that would keep a lesser man than Gillan looking over his shoulder.

A creditable first tour show from what will become a major band, despite the fact that on this occasion most of the applause was drawn for "oldies" like Child In Time.

Support group Strapps gave a good account of themselves, too.

BOB MULLETT

Ian Gillan - 23rd May 1977

The rock blast

Ted Nugent, Odeon, New Street.

TED NUGENT is a musical form of grievous bodily harm . . .

Or, to put it another way, he would make any member of the Noise Abatement Society break down and cry.

For he is without doubt the loudest man in the world. Five minutes of Nugent and it felt like my eardrums were about to burst.

I use the term 'music' in the loosest sense. Nugent uses his guitar like a machine gun, which spits out a succession of notes of blistering intensity.

The musical 'bullets' cascade off the walls, magnifying still further the already frightening noise.

Yet, while I was sure that brain damage was about to develop, it seemed that few, if any of the audience were similarly worried. In fact, to my amazement, they seemed to be enjoying it all.

This adds weight to Nugent's own theory that rock music is enjoyable, but very loud rock is really exciting. By the ecstatic reaction which greeted some of Nugent's numbers, he obviously has a point.

But, having listened to his records, and found them interesting and exciting — with the volume at a normal level — surely Mr. Nugent and his band would command an even bigger following if they compromised just a little.

KEN LAWRENCE

Ted Nugent - 18th Aug 1977

298

High Priests of ear-bashing!

*Judas Priest,
Odeon,
Birmingham*

ABOUT 200 people charged to the front of the stage.

I thought the ice cream lady had arrived. She hadn't. All that happened was the lights had gone out and Judas Priest had come on.

Heads waved trance-like. Arms punched the air as Rob Halford launched into "Exciter" from Priest's new album "Stained Class," released last Friday,

After blasting us with "The Ripper," then "Savage", lead singer Halford asked the faithful: "What's wrong with Birmingham tonight, you're very quiet?"

"Well, they weren't, but Judas Priest would have had difficulty hearing a 21-gun salute over the racket they were making.

I turned down the offer of two pieces of cotton wool from a wise fan beside me, and I moved to the back of the auditorium.

It was just as bad.

The noise level was appalling.

Disciples of the Priest loved it.

TONY McKINSTRY

Judas Priest - 11th February 1978

Rush of excitement to the brain

Rush,
Odeon,
New Street, Birmingham.

FOR A CANADIAN band, Rush play pretty good British rock music.

They could, in fact, be a heavier version of British supergroups like Yes and Genesis. Yet Rush are no three-man copycat act.

They are merely more sophisticated and thoughtful about their music than the great majority of heavy rock bands from across the Atlantic. Most of these are too brash and gimmicky for British audiences.

Rush, in fact, appeared to be just another loud rock band on their last visit here. But they have developed into a highly stylised, exciting group who though obviously influenced by Yes and Genesis, are breaking new ground for themselves.

Neil Peart (drums), Geddy Lee (bass) and Alex Lifeson (lead guitar) are still relatively unknown in Britain. But last night's excellent performance, with a tremendous lights show to add extra atmosphere, had the sell-out audience on their feet throughout.

Their music was fast, pulsating and, above all, memorable.

KEN LAWRENCE

Rush - 12th Feb 1978

POP REVIEWS

Light fantastic
—and music too!

Blue Oyster Cult, Odeon, Birmingham

SO FAR, 1978 has been the year of the light show.

Nowadays, it is not enough just to play the music — there has to be a visual side to the entertainment.

Last night's Blue Oyster Cult show was the best I've seen yet. At times the stage resembled the mothership from "Close Encounters," and throughout the evening vivid laser lights arrowed around the hall.

Their brand of rock 'n' roll is not for the faint hearted. This five - piece New York group let us have it at breath-taking pace right from the start, and didn't let up until the final crescendo, a glorious rendering of the classic "Born To Be Wild"

But this was anything but the only high spot. When Albert Bouchard was left on stage with his drums, another boring solo seemed imminent. But the next

With the laser lights now swirling through the audience.

And the rest of the band returned to finish off "Godzilla" in champion style.

Blue Oyster Cult are like a grittier yet more sophisticated version of Status Quo. While enjoying supergroup status in America, their following in Britain is still growing.

KEN LAWRENCE

Blue Oyster Cult - 1st May 1978

301

Electric shock
to the senses

AC/DC,
Odeon, Birmingham.

I almost drove past the Odeon this morning . . . just to see if it was still standing.

Last night it was subjected to such a violent assault of noise, it could well have been reduced to a pile of rubble.

AC DC brought their brand of high voltage rock to the home of heavy metal . . . the same Midlands that produced Led Zeppelin and Black Sabbath. So to win over such an audience this Aussie five-piece had better be darn good.

Testimony to that was a chanting crowd near hysteria long before the band started to pulverise the eardrums.

As the lights went down, a mass surge took thousands to the front, to girate frantically in time with the pulsating drums of Phill Rudd and the perfectly in-step bass of Cliff Williams.

Outfront singer Bon Scott screeches inaudible vocals into the mike while the crowd's hero, lead guitarist Angus Young, thrashes around the stage, demented.

Their style is way out of date. Zeppelin were doing this years ago but the crowd — and I say crowd because it looked more like the Holte End than a concert audience— were not bothered with the finer points . . . they were there to have their senses smashed with the most powerful rock band I have heard.

PAUL WALKER

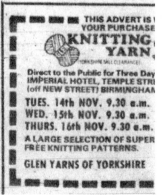

THIS ADVERT IS YOUR PURCHASE

KNITTING YARN

YORKSHIRE SALE CLEARANCE

Direct to the Public for Three Day
IMPERIAL HOTEL, TEMPLE STR
(off NEW STREET) BIRMINGHAM

TUES. 14th NOV. 9.30 a.m.
WED. 15th NOV. 9.30 a.m.
THURS. 16th NOV. 9.30 a.m.

A LARGE SELECTION OF SUPER
FREE KNITTING PATTERNS.

GLEN YARNS OF YORKSHIRE

Nothing changes

Alvin Lee,
Odeon, New Street,
Birmingham.

TEN years ago Alvin Lee was the lead guitarist with Ten Years After — one of the biggest names in rock music.

Now it's Ten Years Later, and as Lee says: "Nothing changes."

He is still the maestro of the late '60s rock, characterised by a strong blues influence, powerful riffs, lots of string-bending, thumping bass and long improvisations that wander into self-indulgence.

There is an excellent cameo from bassist Mick Hawksworth, and even a drum solo from Tom Compton

Naturally enough these are only intervals in the Alvin Lee show. Lee is at his best on extended blues like Sonny Boy Williamson's "Help Me" in which he bottlenecks to the manner born and plays a stunning harmonica.

TOM REID

10 Years Later - 26th November 1979

303

Maiden make it warm

Iron Maiden,
Odeon, New Street.

FOR a sixth-month-old band on their first major tour, Iron Maiden earned the roaring reception they won from Birmingham fans.

But the nuts and bolts of their stage act still need work.

While the five-man band brought some welcome fresh ideas to a heavy metal performance, the tight sound that marked their first album was often missing on stage.

Technical hitches marred parts of their show.

But for the fans, the sheer excitement of the set more than made up for its faults.

Some of the slower tracks such as *Remember Tomorrow* showed Maiden at their best, with impressive lead guitar work from Dennis Stratton.

And by the time the band pounded into *Phantom of the Opera* several fans were storming the stage amid defening calls for encores.

JACKIE BAILEY

Iron Maiden - 7th June 1980

304